Blessings to you & yours!

Love Echoed Back

I Cried Out; He Answered

E LAINE A. L ANKFORD

Elaine A. Lankford

WESTBOW®
PRESS
A DIVISION OF THOMAS NELSON
& ZONDERVAN

Front cover photo by Natalie Kent, Natalie Kent Photography.
Cross illustration by Madeline K. Rhodes.

WestBow Press books may be ordered through booksellers or by contacting:

WestBow Press
A Division of Thomas Nelson & Zondervan
1663 Liberty Drive
Bloomington, IN 47403
www.westbowpress.com
1 (866) 928-1240

ISBN: 978-1-4908-4578-4 (sc)
ISBN: 978-1-4908-4579-1 (hc)
ISBN: 978-1-4908-4577-7 (e)

Library of Congress Control Number: 2014913172

Printed in the United States of America.

WestBow Press rev. date: 8/25/2014

In loving memory of my father, Nathaniel Aston, who taught me love is more than words. I would not be the person I am today without the fine example he set every day I had with him. Even now, I hold on dearly to the memories of my childhood and the man who demonstrated, to many around him, the grace and mercy of our heavenly Father.

Then the LORD reached out and touched my mouth and said, "Look, I have put my words in your mouth!"
—Jeremiah 1:9 NLT

Contents

FOREWORD

Perhaps one of the greatest myths that permeates the minds of those who follow Jesus is "Christians are supposed to be happy and life is supposed to be easy." When you say yes to Jesus, everything just goes better, the sun comes out, the gentle breeze is always at our backs, and the smiles on our faces are hard to wipe off. I'm not sure where this myth came from or why it is so widely accepted as truth, but I do know that many have concluded that Christianity doesn't work when their lives take an unwelcomed turn.

The truth is, life is hard. It's hard for those who follow Jesus, and it's hard for those who don't. For those who choose to go through life with Jesus, however, they can be sure that He will never leave them, even when times are tough.

As a pastor, I have watched countless people start following Jesus only to find that their problems did not go away automatically. I have seen the shell-shocked look on people's faces as they have encountered unexpected tragedies and difficulties. I have lost count of the number of people who have decided that following Jesus simply isn't worth it, and they have walked away from their faith and the church.

I'm excited to have this book, *Love Echoed Back,* to pass on to those who are struggling to follow Jesus when life is hard. It contains the story of Elaine Lankford, a member of my church, and one of those people who has chosen to follow Jesus through life even when it's messy. Although her plans in life were carefully planned out and executed, when she found herself confronting problem after problem, including in her professional and family life, rather than give up, she clung to her faith more tightly than ever.

In this book, you will not only discover that you aren't alone in your struggle, but Elaine has also captured valuable lessons learned and insights into faith and God's character that will encourage you in your own journey. I'm excited to recommend this book to you. I hope in reading it you will make the decision to not give up on your faith when you enter the storms of life.

Blessings,
Jamey Stuart
Senior Pastor
Believers Church
Chesapeake, Virginia

Acknowledgments

To all the pastors and teachers that contributed to my spiritual awakening and growth. Their teachings and written works inspired me to reach beyond what I could see and find a faith that truly glorifies God.

To my Believers Church family for their unwavering encouragement and prayers.

To Beth, for the purest and most honest friendship I have ever known.

To Jamey, Janice, and Kelly for giving so much of their time and support.

To my husband and my son for supporting me throughout the last several years and for loving me as I dream again.

To my Lord and Savior, Jesus Christ, who opened my eyes to life at its finest.

I am forever grateful.

INTRODUCTION

~My Heart to Yours~

The LORD says, "I will guide you along the best
pathway for your life. I will advise you and watch
over you."
—Psalm 32:8 NLT

One of my favorite movies growing up was the 1939 classic film *The Wizard of Oz*. Based on the written work of L. Frank Baum, most people remember this famous children's story. It surrounds a band of unlikely characters who set out to find answers in their time of need. At an impressionable age, I watched the underlying theme involving the forces of good and evil dance across the screen of my television, where good always conquered evil. At the center of the movie was the Land of Oz, a mystical place where dreams came true through the powers of the great and mighty Oz. Initially, what held my attention was the Emerald City, where life was grand, every day was cheerful and exciting, and the residents lived in what appeared to be perfect harmony.

We relate to the Emerald City because we all want that type of life—a life of ease, a life of comfort. Conversely, the wicked witches of the East and West remind us that underneath the everyday comings and goings of life, there is a force working against us; a force that given the chance, ultimately wishes to destroy us. Fortunately for us, unlike the wizard of Oz, whose powers were exaggerated by smoke and mirrors, we actually have a great and powerful Savior, Jesus Christ, the Son of God. He oversees all creation and can assist us in our times of need.

> Finally, be strong in the Lord and in his mighty power. Put on the full armor of God, so that you can take your stand against the devil's schemes. For our struggle is not against flesh and blood, but against the rulers, against the authorities, against the powers of this dark world and against the spiritual forces of evil in the heavenly realms. (Eph. 6:10–12 NIV)

The world would have us believe life is a gamble; it is up to fate; it happens by chance. Life is actually the finest piece of patchwork created by the One who holds the universe. Each patch represents an experience, and each patch holds its own meaning. The rough patches represent those areas of life that nag, tear, and push us to our limits. They refine our characters. The smooth patches represent the good stuff, the things that thrill and overjoy us. We all want a life full of smoothness, but the reality is without the rough spots, we don't fully appreciate the easier times.

Scripture brings to light that life is really a series of choices and consequences. Most of the time, we are responsible for making our own decisions, but there are times when others make them for us. They are the reflection of truth or untruth. The ripple effect can be tragic, especially if we are on the receiving end of someone else's bad choices. Nevertheless, we know Jesus is in control (Prov. 16:9 NKJV). So why does He allow these types of things to happen? Because of His gift of free will (Gen. 2:8–9, 15–17 NKJV). It is up to the individual person to decide whether or not they are going to hurt us, and it is up to us to decide whether or not we are going to forgive. How then do we prepare for these situations or change the outcome? The truth is, sometimes we can't. What we can do is control our reactions to situations and our outlooks on the end results.

> *What we can do is control our reactions to situations and our outlooks on the end results.*

> Consider it pure joy, my brothers and sisters, whenever you face trials of many kinds, because you know that the testing of your faith produces perseverance. Let perseverance finish its work so that you may be mature and complete, not lacking anything. (James 1:2–4 NIV)

This can be the hardest lesson we learn, but Jesus uses tough, tiresome, and tender situations to build us, strengthen us, and prepare us for new avenues in life. It is not always apparent, but if we can stick with it, the payoff can be bigger than we ever imagined.

> Blessed is the one who perseveres under trial because, having stood the test, that person will receive the crown of life that the Lord has promised to those who love him. (James 1:12 NIV)

My journey with Christ started consciously at age eleven. I grew up in a traditional home, a conventional church, and had a relatively normal life, for the most part. It was later in life when the challenges came, the challenges that would draw me closer and tighter to Him, to the point that I would not just know of Him, but I would really *know* Him. Jesus, unlike the wizard of Oz, doesn't desire only to fix your problem; He yearns to fix you. He wants to create a strength within you to carry you not for a moment, but for life. He can use any situation to accomplish His will and bring you through a transformation beyond your understanding. My heart's desire is to inspire anyone and everyone who feels they are struggling in life —there is hope. No matter your struggle, you are not alone. There is someone watching over you.

> In this world, everyone is expendable; however, though Jesus, everyone is redeemable.

Dear God

Help my unbelief,
>*my discouraged heart.*

Help me reposition myself,
>*see the vision You have set before me,*
>*walk through the doors You have opened.*

Help me draw close,
>*stay on the path,*
>*stay the course.*

Help me soar, run, and walk.

Help me feel Your love,
>*receive Your love,*
>*give Your love.*

Help me meditate on,
>*memorize,*
>*and live out Your Word.*

Help me to notice,
>*commit to memory,*
>*appreciate,*
>*and reflect on the little things.*

Help me keep up,
>*keep going,*
>*keep striving,*
>*keep rising.*

Help me in good times,
>*in bad times,*
>*in quiet times,*
>*in chaotic times.*

Help me find peace,
>*find beauty,*
>*find closure,*
>*find sanity.*

Help me grab for the Rock,
        grasp for the Rock,
        hold tight to the Rock.
Help me to stand,
        to fall,
        to kneel,
        to bow down.
Help me to speak,
        to cry out,
        to pray,
        to be silent.
Help me, Father God,
        Son of God,
        Holy Spirit of God.
Help me read Your Word,
        understand Your Word,
        find revelation in Your Word.
Help me realize my sin,
        repent of my sin,
        not repeat my sin.
Help me speak forth the Word,
        whisper the Word,
        shout the Word,
        repeat the Word,
        proclaim the Word again and again.
Help me overcome yesterday's sorrow,
        experience today's joy,
        expect tomorrow's blessings.

CHAPTER 1

Spiritual Oz
~This Isn't Kansas~

Job continued his discourse: "How I long for the
months gone by, for the days when God watched
over me, when his lamp shone on my head and by
his light I walked through darkness!"
—Job 29:1–3 NIV

L et me quickly set the stage. With my heart surrendered to
Christ at a tender age, I forged ahead in life. By sixth grade,
I felt led by the Lord to enter the profession of nursing once I
finished school. Therefore, with iron determination, I set my
focus on this goal and never looked back. The spirit of nursing
has always been compatible with demonstrating the love of
Jesus. It is among a handful of professions able to provide
unconditional support, hope, and regard for people as human
beings. The soft touch of a compassionate nurse has long been
compared to being caressed by an angel. I would go further
to say it is a touch from the healing hand of Christ. Nurses not
only have access to the human mind and body, but are by far
among the few who see beyond the wounds, scars, and tears

into the depth of the soul. We are privileged to be among those in which people feel comfortable enough to open up and cry out for help on all levels of need, whether physical, emotional, or mental. Anyone practicing in this profession should regard this role as sacred.

After climbing the professional ladder and transitioning from a registered nurse to a nurse practitioner, I could see yet another facet to human suffering. Beyond the diagnosis, beyond the lab and X-ray results, beyond the initial complaint, one needs to seek a root cause for the person's situation. From this perspective, the connection between human suffering and spiritual issues was undeniable, and it challenged me to go deeper in seeking answers to life.

Upon completing training as a nurse practitioner, I pursued my passion of working within the field of pain management. Here I was, as they say, in the zone. Here, caring for hurting people, I felt I was accomplishing not only a professional ambition, but a life mission as well. It doesn't take long, working with chronic pain patients, to realize that their physical pain is often wrapped in emotional or mental stress and sometimes, unknown to them, spiritual discomfort. "In 1931, the French medical missionary Dr. Albert Schweitzer wrote, 'Pain is a more terrible lord of mankind than even death itself.'"[1] This is incredibly true. It was my great honor and privilege to work with these individuals suffering from various chronic pain states and bring a little of Christ's love and light to them in a practical way.

Sharing God's Word and the love of Jesus is our highest calling in life. I pray the medical and nursing professions don't lose this focus. Within this age of technology and advancement, hospitals and offices become more secular by the day. Because of the lengths we will go to save the human body, the human soul and spirit are pushed into the background. It must become our passion to bring them back to the forefront. Sharing one's faith can lead to some very tender moments between provider and patient. Most patients appreciate the thoughtfulness behind it, as it shows the provider is interested in them in a true and sincere manner. I am not advocating pushing one's faith upon another; I simply encourage those of faith to be looking for a door, a window of opportunity. If we are truly looking, there is usually one to be found.

Father God, I have heard You calling to feed the hungry, clothe the naked, care for the sick. May my steps this day travel the right road. May my eyes see the individual before me and discern the correct need. May my hands be an extension of Yours, comforting the soul and spirit. May my ears pick up the clues that will unravel the diagnosis. May my mind carefully calculate the strategy for excelled healing and be combined with Your supernatural power. May my heart flow with compassion and empathy in a world growing cold. May this individual before me see only a living reflection of You and Your love before them. In Jesus' name, I pray. Amen.

Yes, I was in my sweet spot as described in *Cure for the Common Life*.

> A zone, a region, a life precinct in which you were made to dwell. He tailored the curves of your life to fit an empty space in his jigsaw puzzle. And life makes sweet sense when you find your spot.
> —Max Lucado [2]

Then, after sixteen years in the nursing profession, putting my best foot forward, walking in integrity and honesty, and caring deeply for the well-being of others, all the good things a Christian should be doing, I got the shock of my life. On August 6, 2008, my whole world changed. The medical practice I had put my heart and soul into was closed, and my supervising physician was suspended from practicing medicine pending a hearing. I would be left unemployed and wondering initially how the bills would be paid. Little did I know, this was the tip of the iceberg, and life would never be the same.

> Be alert and of sober mind. Your enemy the devil prowls around like a roaring lion looking for someone to devour. (1 Peter 5:8 NIV)

Though I had come to a deeper understanding of Jesus and what it was like to be in a genuine relationship with Him a few years earlier, I suddenly realized all the ground I had gained and all the faith that had been built was about to be tested. Soon, this minuscule event on the road of life turned into a massive mountain of volcanic smoke and ash taking direct aim at all I knew to be true. In the short run, my husband and I supplemented our fleeting income with a small amount of money given to us by my parents. I was hopeful that the charges against my employer would be dropped, and things would get back to normal around the first of the year.

In September, however, I found myself in the middle of a professional attack clearly motivated by politics and built on false allegations. This was the beginning of the most trying time in my life. Reeling from the potential outcome, forced to hire an attorney, and the bills piling up, life became overwhelming. As the days went by, the task of defending myself became all-consuming. There had to be attention to the smallest detail. It was during this time that Jesus began to work in me. I was so used to Him working through me, I found Him working in me to be quite different. Confusing. Saddening. Anxiety producing. Point blank, uncomfortable. Although there were times I could not see the way out, I knew He was there. Although extreme emotions pushed and pulled at me, I knew He would not leave me.

Surviving the Initial Attack

Nothing could have prepared us for the events to come, but in times of trouble, one has to have an anchor in order to survive, and anchored we were.

> So God has given both his promise and his oath. These two things are unchangeable because it is impossible for God to lie. Therefore, we who have fled to him for refuge can have great confidence as we hold to the hope that lies before us. This hope is a strong and trustworthy anchor for our souls. (Heb. 6:18–19 NLT)

Looking back now, having survived the stress and the strain of what can only be described as utter chaos all around us, I realize that the Lord began to prepare me for this time of testing a few years earlier. I am convinced the choices my devoted husband and I made then started a process in us that He built upon day by day, until a foundation was laid so strong, He could begin to take us to the next level in God's plan for us. The most noteworthy choice we made was to step out in faith, to leave religion behind, and seek a true relationship with our Savior. We left the security of the traditional church setting and found Jesus. Had we not made the move to our current church, we may have fallen victim to the traps and snares laid in our path. By going outside our comfort zone, we found life with Jesus the way it was meant to be—a full-time relationship. We gained perspective, and we found strength.

> *The most noteworthy choice we made was to step out in faith, to leave religion behind, and seek true relationship with our Savior.*

One of our newfound passions was participating in small groups. Just as the name implies, anyone seeking answers to everyday life situations is invited to engage in the study of God's Word on a more intimate level with ten to fifteen others. Small group becomes an extension of the larger church gathering, and it mimics the way the first Christians not only shared their faith, but also grew steadfast in it.

> All the believers devoted themselves to the apostles' teaching, and to fellowship, and to sharing in meals (including the Lord's Supper), and to prayer. (Acts 2:42 NLT)

After participating in several small groups, we began to lead a small group. We went from sitting in service, feeding on the Word, to living it out every single day. We went from having a few friends to having an extended family devoted to meeting each other's needs. Every Friday night from September to about May, you will find us surrounded by those who love Jesus, and a few who are seeking Him. The Lord has blessed us many times over and ministered to us through this outreach of the church. We are humbled and honored by those who come to our home and simply do life together. It was through small group that we could talk honestly about what was happening to us, seek answers, and find acceptance and love through a very bitter battle for justice.

In addition, Jesus spoke to us through the Bible studies we explored. During the initial months of questioning and probing by my professional peers, our church corporately and within each small group, took the New Testament Challenge. The challenge was to read through the entire New Testament in sixty-three days. This could not have come at a better time. What would Jesus say to us, what did we need to learn? As I read through the New Testament that fall, Jesus began to speak to me and give me different Scriptures that strengthened me along the way. I trust by sharing the central themes He revealed to me, you will find the same boldness in faith that I experienced. I desire more than anything that you see a God that stands ready to shower you with His love and blessings.

Finding True Comfort in the Middle of a Crisis

> Praise be to the God and Father of our Lord Jesus Christ, *the Father of compassion and the God of all comfort, who comforts us in all our troubles,* so that we can comfort those in any trouble with the comfort we ourselves receive from God. (2 Cor. 1:3–4 NIV, italics mine)

Have you ever had someone try to comfort you, yet even with the best of intentions, you knew that they had no clue what you were going through or at least you thought they didn't? We have a Father in heaven who is full of compassion and eager to comfort us. Either we feel His direct comfort through the Holy Spirit, or He sends people into our lives that bring us comfort. Scripture teaches us that there are those who can relate because even though their struggles may not be exactly the same as ours, everyone suffers at some point. It could be grief, defeat, betrayal, or anger. No matter what the cause, we all feel and go through the same emotions. During these times of distress, we can choose to be self-indulgent, or we can choose to refocus our energy on someone else. The latter, I would learn, is the best path to self-healing.

Gaining Peace from the One True Source

> Rejoice in the Lord always. I will say it again: Rejoice!
> Let your gentleness be evident to all. The Lord is near.
> Do not be anxious about anything, but in every situation,
> by prayer and petition, with thanksgiving, present
> your requests to God. *And the peace of God, which
> transcends all understanding, will guard your hearts and
> your minds in Christ Jesus.* (Phil. 4:4–7 NIV, italics mine)

You can have unexplainable peace in the most volatile times.
There are truly no words able to accurately describe it. There
is no image that can justifiably portray its power. You just know
it when it washes over you. God is waiting for you to ask Him
for anything, for everything. He is looking for those who pursue
Him joyfully no matter the circumstance. He is looking for faith,
so that He may release incredible coverings of peace.

Enduring the Challenge Before You

> Consider it pure joy, my brothers and sisters, whenever
> you face trials of many kinds, because you know
> that *the testing of your faith produces perseverance.*
> Let perseverance finish its work so that you may be
> mature and complete, not lacking anything. (James
> 1:2–4 NIV, italics mine)

There is worth to any situation that befalls us. God uses hard
situations for various purposes. In order for us to grow in our
walk, we must be trained. The objective of resistance training
is endurance. The muscle of faith can only be strengthened
when we are fighting against something. We must be relentless
to see it through to reach our spiritual goals.

Humility Trumps Pride

> *Humble yourselves*, therefore, under God's mighty
> hand, *that he may lift you up in due time.* Cast all your
> anxiety on him because he cares for you. (1 Peter
> 5:6–7 NIV, italics mine)

The Bible never says we are without responsibility in a matter. It
doesn't say God is on our timetable. It doesn't say He might get
around to us. It tells us to come to Him without arrogance, and in
due time, He will set us apart from the things that weigh us down.

Finding Eternal Things by Living through Temporal Things

> We are hard pressed on every side, but not crushed;
> perplexed, but not in despair; persecuted, but not
> abandoned; struck down, but not destroyed … *For
> our light and momentary troubles are achieving for us
> an eternal glory* that far outweighs them all. So we fix
> our eyes not on what is seen, but on what is unseen,
> since what is seen is temporary, but what is unseen
> is eternal. (2 Cor. 4:8–9, 17–18 NIV, italics mine)

We are made for eternal purposes, and our experiences show
us our true makeups. Are you convinced that what lies in front
of you is too hard, too monumental to be overcome? Most
people feel they can do anything in the short run if there is a
light at the end of the tunnel. On the other hand, what if the end
is not so visible? If we refocus our perspective on the larger
picture and measure everything by eternity, we quickly realize
how small the things of this world are. In the grand scheme of
things, God is working something out in you. Allow Jesus to

reveal those things to you. Everything in life is temporary, but everything with Christ is eternal.

Learning to Let the Pain and Suffering of a Trial Work

> Submit yourselves for the Lord's sake to every human authority: whether to the emperor, as the supreme authority, or to governors, who are sent by him to punish those who do wrong and to commend those who do right. *For it is God's will that by doing good you should silence the ignorant talk of foolish people.* Live as free people, but do not use your freedom as a cover-up for evil; live as God's slaves. Show proper respect to everyone, love the family of believers, fear God, honor the emperor … *For it is commendable if someone bears up under the pain of unjust suffering because they are conscious of God.* But how is it to your credit if you receive a beating for doing wrong and endure it? But if you suffer for doing good and you endure it, this is commendable before God. *To this you were called, because Christ suffered for you, leaving you an example, that you should follow in his steps.* (1 Peter 2:13–17, 19–21 NIV, italics mine)

We are called to be representatives of Christ's nature, even in the face of pain and suffering. Submission to authority is an incredible thing. It does not come naturally or easily. Our very nature wants to rise up against it. Our need to defend ourselves is intoxicating. Even so, our best defense of ourselves is only as strong as God's weakest effort to protect us. We were not meant to fight these battles alone, but to have faith in the One who is full of justice and sees all we go through. No one has ever suffered more at the hands of others than Jesus did, yet the Bible tells us "He opened not His mouth" (Isa. 53:7 NKJV).

Trusting in the Law of Sowing and Reaping

> Do not be deceived: God cannot be mocked. *A man reaps what he sows* ... Let us not become weary in doing good, for at the proper time we will reap a harvest if we do not give up. (Gal. 6:7, 9 NIV, italics mine)

Throughout the Bible, people of little importance to those of massive influence have belittled the God of the universe. All have fallen. We celebrate a *big* God. Our lives are not a surprise to Him. He can discern the inner heart. We may not always have an easy life, but we cannot really begin to wrap our minds around an existence without Him. Even those who reject Him by rejecting Jesus cannot truly appreciate life cut off from Him. In this life, He never stops pursuing them, and He is always there waiting for them. How we define our existence in relation to God, *decisions plus actions*, fuels an activity that occurs constantly, *sowing produces reaping*. Those who love God and pursue His path will not always have the easiest path. Our sincerity in pursuing His will, regardless of our circumstances, catches God's eye. Even when we feel relief, reward, or recognition is not coming, we need only to wait a little longer. God will make all things right in time.

Relying on His Protection

> To him who is able *to keep you from stumbling* and to present you before his glorious presence without fault and with great joy— to the only God our Savior be glory, majesty, power and authority, through Jesus Christ our Lord, before all ages, now and forevermore! Amen. (Jude 1:24–25 NIV, italics mine)

We will never truly understand all the things that God protects us from in this life. Even when times are bad, we cannot grasp the big picture of what Christ is shielding us from had we not been in relationship with Him. Probably not until we reach heaven will we truly appreciate the destruction that could have befallen us had Jesus not been holding us in His hands.

As I devoured the New Testament, there was no doubt that these verses were soaked deeply in by my spirit, due to the circumstances within which I found myself. These verses spoke truth. These verses gave hope. These verses were power. God's Word is alive; it contains everything you need to arm yourself in every situation. You need only to open this book, this love letter from God, to find infinite grace and mercy. It was no accident that during this time of unrest in my life, the New Testament was covered so intensely. My Bible is now full of highlights and tabs, marking these verses and others. I would find myself reading and rereading them, speaking them aloud, and meditating on them in the weeks and months to come. I am grateful that we covered the New Testament. Jesus used this challenge to get me through a tough situation. It kept me focused on Him because I forced myself to sit each night before going to bed and read the Scripture assigned for that day. I did not and would not let anything get in the way of reading my Bible. I knew if I was going to have a breakthrough in my situation, I needed to be faithful to the New Testament Challenge. It was a significant building block in my faith. To experience the Creator of the universe speaking into my situation, to feel Him reaching out to me page after page, just blew me away. Clearly, it was exactly what I needed. No one can match His orchestration of timing. It is undeniably perfect. That is just how He is; always on time!

Protection
Sowing and Reaping
Pain and Suffering
Eternal Perspective
Humility
Endurance
Peace
Comfort
CRISIS

The Door

I know You are there on the other side of this door.
The door that keeps me locked in and You locked out.
This door is different.
Its parts must be seen spiritually, not physically felt.
The keyhole, the doorknob, the hinges are
not visible to the casual passerby.
To them, it is a wall, never to be passed through.

However, I know it is but a door; nonetheless, it challenges me.
If I can see the keyhole, then I can start to glance at the other side
where You stand; where You wait.
I can then start to dream, imagine, and wonder
about what You have in store.
If I can see the doorknob, then I can begin to toy with the idea
You have planted in my heart.
What will I do when I'm on the other side?
How long will You wait?

Ahhh, the hinges, now there is the trick.
For the keyhole is just a tiny hole, the doorknob round and cold
—but the hinges, they are my salvation.
With each tiny hinge comes freedom.
With each tiny hinge comes ability.
With each tiny hinge, the way out becomes clear.
Because with the tiny hinges the door swings open wide.

No more will this door trap me.
No more will this door block me.
No more will this door imprison me.
Because now that I am on the other side, I realize
You were never really blocked from entering.
You just preferred that I peep through the keyhole,
that I turn the doorknob,
and I use the hinges to swing the door of my heart open wide.

CHAPTER 2

When the Rain Lasts All Day and All Night
~Your Hair Will Be Frizzy~

There is a time for everything, and a season for every activity under the heavens:

> a time to be born and a time to die,
> a time to plant and a time to uproot,
> a time to kill and a time to heal,
> a time to tear down and a time to build,
> a time to weep and a time to laugh,
> a time to mourn and a time to dance,
> a time to scatter stones and a time to gather them,
> a time to embrace and a time to refrain from embracing,
> a time to search and a time to give up,
> a time to keep and a time to throw away,
> a time to tear and a time to mend,
> a time to be silent and a time to speak,
> a time to love and a time to hate,
> a time for war and a time for peace.
>
> —Ecclesiastes 3:1–8 (NIV)

You have no doubt heard the expression when it rains it pours. Three months into my ordeal, no job, and living off half our usual income, I experienced a flash flood. Just two weeks prior to facing those who stood in judgment of me, everything that could go wrong did. My eldest aunt, whom I dearly loved, was hospitalized due to a massive stroke. It was fatal, and we lost her the day before Thanksgiving. On Thanksgiving Day, we found out that our credit card number had been stolen and suspicious charges placed on our account. There I sat, on a day that in years past had been filled with sweet memories, saddened by the loss of my aunt and going through the aggravation of cancelling our credit card due to fraud. Two days later, we got a call from a couple in New York and a man in Texas wanting to verify their good fortune. They each received two eight hundred dollar money orders with our names attached as the sender. Within forty-eight hours, we were the victims of both credit card fraud and identity theft. What was going on? Then the fuel pump on my husband's truck went out, leaving us with an unexpected bill to pay. Could this be happening now? Next, my cell phone screen malfunctioned, and I had to replace my cell phone, yet another charge. To end this perfect storm of stress, the right front light on our car burned out and had to be replaced. Seriously? All this in less than a two-week time period, I lost it that day. Normally, the trivial events that occurred would have been aggravating at best, but all meshed on top of a major crisis, they became the proverbial straw that broke the camel's back. I thought, *What else, Lord, what else? I can't do this anymore; I need you!*

I cried on my husband's shoulder that night, and as I sat sulking, an old memory regarding a job promotion came back to me. I had planned on that promotion, prayed for that promotion, was actually told I would receive that promotion, only to have the offer taken away at the last minute. I came home and went to a small clearing in our backyard where there was a tree stump at the edge of the woods. Sitting on that stump, I would cry out to Jesus. Defeated and with tears flowing, I questioned Him as to the meaning of such a disappointment. Silence. Little did I know as I sat there focused on the short term that several months later, a better position, a more independent position, would come along, and I would be the only person in the hospital who could fill it!

> Now this I know: The LORD gives victory to his anointed. He answers him from his heavenly sanctuary with the victorious power of his right hand. (Ps. 20:6 NIV)

Recalling that memory initially brought no comfort. There I was crying out again. In that moment of exhaustion, all I could do was compare how much *more* this hurt than back then. I felt like I was sitting on that stump again, full of disappointment and watching my dreams go up in smoke. And then it dawned on me; Jesus is faithful. He "*is* the same yesterday, today, and forever" (Heb. 13:8 NKJV). If Jesus had such a wonderful plan for me after that dark period of time, what might He have prepared for me now? Was I actually fighting Him? Was there something He was trying to get through to me, and I was being stubborn again just like on the stump? I began to cheer up and look with expectancy. There is invariably a point when we have to release the situation to Christ so that He can work through us and for us, because His plans are always better.

> However, as it is written: "What no eye has seen, what no ear has heard, and what no human mind has conceived"— the things God has prepared for those who love him. (1 Cor. 2:9 NIV)

In early December, the night before the scheduled meeting, we drove up to the surrounding area and spent the night. I wasn't nervous, per se, just anxious for the matter to be over and settled. I had asked the Lord when the time came to provide peace within my spirit and the words to say. That morning when I got up, I felt tremendous peace. It truly passed all understanding and it stayed with me throughout the long morning wait, prior to and during the interview. I felt comfortable during the questioning, and when I made my final remarks, I knew He had given me the words to say because they just flowed out. We drove home that day, and I was totally satisfied that the situation was in the hands of Jesus.

> Because of the LORD's great love we are not consumed, for his compassions never fail. They are new every morning; great is your faithfulness. I say to myself, "The LORD is my portion; therefore I will wait for him." The LORD is good to those whose hope is in him, to the one who seeks him; it is good to wait quietly for the salvation of the LORD. (Lam. 3:22–26 NIV)

As it were, due to the process of information review, no answer was given the day of the hearing. I left expecting a response concerning my case prior to Christmas. It didn't come, only silence. Christmas arrived without any resolution. More silence. Then life took yet another turn. Christmas Day we had the entire family over as always—my parents, my in-laws, my brother and his wife, my nephew, and us. Christmas lunch, Christmas presents, and Christmas laughs; all and all, it was a good day. After leaving our house, my parents made the trip over to my brother's house just a few miles away to give my nephew time to show off his gifts from Santa. My parents were always good about giving equal time to the grandsons. Unfortunately, Christmas night didn't end the way it was supposed to; it didn't end like so many Christmas nights before. This time it ended in a car accident just up the road from my brother's house. My mom came through with some bruises; my dad suffered a small fracture in his sternum. The sternum is the thick, hard bone running down the center of one's chest. My dad, at the time, was seventy-nine years old, suffered from a chronic lung disorder, and was using oxygen on a daily basis. Due to the fracture, which by all accounts was small, he was sent to a local trauma center for observation.

My father was a gentle, soft-spoken man, but able to defend family and friend when necessary. A proud Korean War veteran, he was tough, and throughout the next two days, although we all knew how much he must have been hurting, he never complained more than to say he was sore. We prayed for his recovery; we thanked Jesus for the fact that he was not injured anymore than he was, and we fully expected to bring him home. The Lord had other plans. In a sudden turn of events, on the second evening of my father's hospital stay, his state of being went from totally active to totally comatose. In a matter of seconds, my dad's heart slowed down and then stopped, forcing the nurses to resuscitate him. He never regained consciousness. When we arrived at the hospital that night to see him, I walked up to his room, unaware of what had just taken place. Then I saw the bed, the place where my father had been, now empty and stripped down. As a nurse, I knew something was terribly wrong. The nursing staff told us about the current events. Incidentally, he had been moved to the intensive care unit. Making our way toward the ICU that night was the longest walk of my life.

You see, my father was the closest thing to my heavenly Father I have ever known. Always there, always ready with a smile, always ready to help if you were in need.

> Gray hair is a crown of glory; it is gained by living a godly life. (Prov. 16:31 NLT)

When we were finally able to see my father, it was a chilling experience. Instead of my father, there was a person hooked up from head to toe on machines of every kind. I had helped many families go through the same situation, but this time, this patient was my father, and the experience was surreal. I remember praying in that instance, *Please God, don't let him linger if you want him. I would rather give him to you quickly than have this go on and on.* We spent the next six hours glued to his bedside, waiting and watching for any glimmer of hope the situation would reverse course and this would pass. Then, in the early-morning hours as I watched the monitors, I saw what I was hoping not to see. His heart was failing again, his blood pressure dropping. I walked my mother out of the room just moments before his heart stopped. The nursing staff was successful in regaining a heartbeat, but I knew when I looked at his countenance afterwards that he wasn't really there. His spirit was, indeed, halfway between this world and heaven. I explained the state of his condition to my mother; we talked with the doctors, and called my brother to return to the hospital. As a family, we made the decision that no family wants to make. We knew it was time for Dad to go home; not to our home, but to his eternal home. We knew his healing was a heartbeat away, but in order to obtain it, he must be released from this physical world we cling to so tightly. We had the life support measures removed, and quietly, with the dignity he deserved, my father went to be with the Lord. As we waited with him for his spirit to depart, all that kept going through my mind was, *Run along now, Dad. We will see you soon.*

When my father died, there wasn't a hole left in my heart, there was a tremendous valley, deep and wide. No matter the loss, Jesus is faithful. In our grief, He was there, and His comfort was discernable. When we got in the car, my husband had the radio playing softly. The first song I heard was "There Will Be a Day" and the words:

> *There will be a day with no more tears, no more pain,*
> *and no more fears*
> *There will be a day when the burdens of this place, will*
> *be no more, we'll see Jesus face to face*
> *But until that day, we'll hold on to you always*[1]

I will never forget the car ride home or the days that followed.

> A good name is better than fine perfume, and the day
> of death better than the day of birth. (Eccl. 7:1 NIV)

In times of confusion, in times of grief, and for every time in between, the Bible provides us with the roadmap to life. When we think we are the only ones who have ever felt the things we feel, it is there to help us understand that we are not alone. As I reflected on the Scriptures during this time, the story of Job stood out and provided reassurance that my troubles and sorrows were well known to almighty God, and I was not forgotten. Job was a good man, and he was blessed with family and fortune. Then instantly, in a matter of hours, everything changed. There was major loss of fortune and family, so much so that he sat in ashes contemplating everything that had happened. Throughout the pages of Job's story, everything was in question, from how he had lived his life, to the true nature of his heart, to his faith in God. He endured a tremendous time of testing. He asked the ultimate question that most of us ask: Why me? Yet, his faith was firmly planted in the Lord.

> Job stood up and tore his robe in grief. Then he
> shaved his head and fell to the ground to worship. He

said, "I came naked from my mother's womb, and I will be naked when I leave. The LORD gave me what I had, and the LORD has taken it away. Praise the name of the LORD!" In all of this, Job did not sin by blaming God. (Job 1:20–22 NLT)

I so related to Job. He held no belief of self-perfection. He simply yearned to do what was right constantly and strived for excellence continuously in all he did. His profession of innocence sounded familiar, and the raw emotions that poured out from his innermost being echoed those I felt. There is a realization that life isn't fair, but God is just. Then there is this beautiful encounter with God, so intimate that Job is overwhelmed by His greatness.

I know that You can do all things, and that no thought *or* purpose of Yours can be restrained *or* thwarted. [You said to me] Who is this that darkens *and* obscures counsel [by words] without knowledge? Therefore [I now see] I have [rashly] uttered what I did not understand, things too wonderful for me, which I did not know … *I had heard of You [only] by the hearing of the ear, but now my [spiritual] eye sees You.* Therefore I loathe [my words] *and* abhor myself and repent in dust and ashes. (Job 42:2–3, 5-6 AB, italics mine)

Just as Job sought an encounter with his Creator, I too was seeking Him. Even so, at the time, I, like Job, had no idea what I was asking.

Soon after the funeral, reality hit again. There was still the looming professional issue to deal with; certainly, Jesus would remove the situation. Weren't the events of the past few months enough, and now my father was gone? One of the Lord's promises is He will never allow more than we can handle (1 Cor. 10:13 NKJV). In truth, what we perceive that we can take versus what we actually can handle with Jesus' help is dramatically different. It quickly became apparent that my perceptions regarding current events and the Lord's were polar opposites. Word soon came the informal process had stalled, and there would indeed be a formal hearing, but no date was set.

> *In truth, what we perceive that we can take versus what we actually can handle with Jesus' help is dramatically different.*

With no guarantee on how long this matter would drag out, I knew I needed to get back to work. I needed to move on. Determined not to be defeated, I pursued a couple of job opportunities that had arisen. The reality was that the practice I worked for was not going to recover from this unfortunate, unbalanced attack and would remain closed. I was going to have to press on. Deeply saddened and gun-shy from all the previous events, I spoke with two prospective employers. I asked Jesus to direct my path, to open only the door I should enter, and close the door I should not. During the next few weeks, one job offer evaporated and the other materialized. Finally, I felt I was getting somewhere, and things were looking up. Then just as I was beginning orientation, word came that there was a snag, and as quickly as the job started, it ended again. What a disappointment. Couldn't I have this one victory? Was God angry with me after all? Every which way I turned, the same dark cloud seemed to overshadow me. Looking back now, I believe Jesus was allowing me a glimpse of where I thought I wanted to be, so as time passed, I would come to realize that instead of reaching forward, I was reaching backwards. Instead of always wondering if the choices I would eventually make were good choices or not, I would understand the progression of my steps.

This latest wrinkle in my saga was brought to the attention of those overseeing my case. The reality of what was happening was setting in, and the truth was that without a clear resolution to the case, it was going to be impossible for me to obtain work in my field again. Now, six months into this process, I was informed that the formal hearing would be delayed, not for a few weeks but for a few months. At this point, I was dizzy. In agony, I remember crying out to Jesus from the depths of my soul, tears streaming down my cheeks relentlessly, but all I could think to do was surrender, *Your will Lord, not mine.*

> I cried out to God for help; I cried out to God to hear me. When I was in distress, I sought the Lord; at night I stretched out untiring hands, and I would not be comforted. I remembered you, God, and I groaned; I meditated, and my spirit grew faint. You kept my eyes from closing; I was too troubled to speak. I thought about the former days, the years of long ago; I remembered my songs in the night. My heart meditated and my spirit asked: "Will the Lord reject forever? Will he never show his favor again? Has his unfailing love vanished forever? Has his promise failed for all time? Has God forgotten to be merciful? Has he in anger withheld his compassion?" … "I will remember the deeds of the LORD; yes, I will remember your miracles of long ago. I will consider all your works and meditate on all your mighty deeds." Your ways, God, are holy. What god is as great as our God? … Your path led through the sea, your way through the mighty waters, *though your footprints were not seen.* (Ps. 77:1–9, 11–13, 19 NIV, italics mine)

There was no going around it; I was headed straight into the eye of the storm, and although I could not make out what He was doing, I knew He was there. I wasn't happy about it, but I knew He was there. I certainly didn't feel strong enough, but I knew He was there. In counseling with my senior pastor, I was given this verse:

> These are the nations the LORD left to test all those Israelites who had not experienced any of the wars in Canaan (he did this only to teach warfare to the descendants of the Israelites who had not had previous battle experience): the five rulers of the Philistines, all the Canaanites, the Sidonians, and the Hivites living in the Lebanon mountains from Mount Baal Hermon to Lebo Hamath. *They were left to test the Israelites to see whether they would obey the LORD's commands,* which he had given their ancestors through Moses. (Judg. 3:1–4 NIV, italics mine)

I mulled over this passage for quite some time. I had come to understand that my faith was being tested, but for what particular purpose, I wasn't sure. Now I felt at least some minor reasoning for the circumstances surrounding me. Over time, I began to understand those most effective in sharing their faith have a testimony to share. I love the definition of testimony: "first hand authentication of a fact."[2] When I looked back over this section of Scripture concerning the Israelites taking the land of Canaan, I realized that much like them, I had yet to fight a true knock-down, drag-out fight. I had grown up in church; I knew the Bible stories; I knew Jesus, but I had not actively had to use my faith, nor learned to lean solely on Him to battle through a true-life crisis. I was in training, and He was not going to let me out of the exercise until I was battleworthy.

> Praise the LORD, who is my rock. He trains my
> hands for war and gives my fingers skill for battle.
> (Ps. 144:1 NLT)

Time continued to pass. It felt like being trapped in a nightmare from which I couldn't wake up. Each passing day only added to the disbelief of how far this was going. Caught in a state of political limbo, an attempt to meet with the opposing side's representative outside of the formal hearing process was worth pursuing. Surely, presentation of the truth meant something. Certainly, the facts cried out for justice.

Just prior to this meeting, I went on a weekend retreat to Rockbridge with the ladies from the church. Located in the beautiful mountains of Virginia, there are a lot of outdoor activities to do, including hiking, rope course crossing, and swimming in the lake. However, it was still early in the year, and the lake was ice-cold. Some of us, feeling adventurous, decided we would brave the elements and go down the slides, taking a quick plunge in the frigid lake water. This was something I had never done in this type of setting, and I was excited for the distraction. I remember the thrill of flying down the long, flexible slide, plunging beneath the ice-cold lake water, and facing the physical challenge of feeling trapped, almost paralyzed beneath the surface. So true to life were these feelings. A brief sense of struggle and suffocation set in due to the extreme cold, but as I emerged from below the water's ceiling, I experienced a different set of emotions— sweet release and then freedom in a way I had never felt them. I had broken through the surface; I had conquered the elements, and I was thrilled. The end was totally worth the beginning, and all I could think was, *There is nothing too hard when I face it with you, Lord.*

As part of the retreat, we gathered to hear words of encouragement from an invited speaker. This particular speaker revisited the story of the Samaritan woman at the well (John 4:4–30 NKJV). Here was a woman despised and rejected, no doubt rumors went on about her all over town, and yet she pushed on the best she knew how. Here was a woman whose life was tangled and twisted by the past, still searching for some type of hope. She would meet Jesus, and in one moment, her whole life would change. This one encounter would be her salvation. Toward the end of their conversation, Jesus would explain the free gift available to all and how those accepting this gift will be known.

> "Woman," Jesus replied, "believe me, a time is coming when you will worship the Father neither on this mountain nor in Jerusalem. You Samaritans worship what you do not know; we worship what we do know, for salvation is from the Jews. *Yet a time is coming and has now come when the true worshipers will worship the Father in the Spirit and in truth, for they are the kind of worshipers the Father seeks. God is spirit, and his worshipers must worship in the Spirit and in truth.*" (John 4:21–24 NIV, italics mine)

Something began to stir in me; where had I been the last few years? Was I ready to be honest with myself and my God that worshiping Him was, in recent times, just becoming a priority in life? Would I let the freedom of the gift I was given so long ago grow and flourish to the point where I could no longer go a day without praising Him? How did my focus go from the simple things in life to this complex drive to accomplish? Seemingly, the answers came in the next session as the speaker spoke on Matthew 3:16–4:11 (NKJV) surrounding the temptation of Jesus in the wilderness, passages we can all relate to in one way or another.

Lust of the Flesh, Lust of the Eye, Pride of Life

Lust of the flesh encases things of a physical nature in which we develop an unhealthy appetite. Soon after starting to work, the temptation to satisfy my physical wants came quickly and without true thought. Eating out, for instance, was a regular event; morning, noon, and night in some cases for sheer convenience. Clothes for different seasons were purchased randomly and spontaneously without regard for need versus want. I felt I deserved these guilty pleasures because I worked hard and earned enough to purchase them, but they were costly in many ways.

Lust of the eyes. The Devil makes huge promises that he can never deliver, but we entertain them nonetheless. We believe we can keep up with the mystical and ever-evolving Joneses. In reality, that constant yearning to be on top is a complete setup. Thus, they become idols, filling our senses to capacity, all the while tearing down the spiritual walls meant to protect us.

Pride of life. This temptation encompasses feelings of mistrust and doubt in what God states. Careers are built on this notion. If I don't do it, no one will do it for me—even Jesus. We either don't believe Jesus will catch us if we fall, or we don't believe He will show up in time. We are just not sure. So we trust in our careers. We trust that they are secure, can make us happy, supply our needs, and we foolishly believe we are potentially nondependent on the Lord.

I would not completely take in the signals Jesus was sending me until I was in a place in life where the enticement could no longer play out. The veil covering my heart was ripping and tearing. It would be painful, but it would cause my spiritual eyes to fly wide open, allowing me to see that somewhere along the way, my good intentions of following Jesus had been masterfully manipulated, and I had allowed myself to be played. The dawning of my freedom from such useless, inefficient living was rapidly approaching, and the battle was on.

> The enemy will not see you vanish into God's company
> without an effort to reclaim you.—C.S. Lewis[3]

Upon returning from Rockbridge, we prepared to meet with the opposing attorney overseeing the case to present the truth again. In a situation like this, it is all you can do. However, thirty minutes into the meeting it was obvious that the other side was too tempted by its political agenda to do the right thing. Regardless of my innocence, I was going to be a casualty in this war. It didn't matter I had obtained an honorable and pristine reputation throughout my nursing career. It didn't matter that there was no one else throwing stones at me. It didn't matter what I had suffered or stood to lose.

And then with pinpoint clarity, I knew that it didn't matter. Whatever they thought or believed, whatever they tried to hang on me, even if they thought they were my source; I knew the truth and the truth would set me free. I know the One who sees my innermost thoughts, the One who searches my heart, the One who calls me His own. I know He is my source, and through Him, I can do all things. In essence, I was experiencing the feelings of Rockbridge all over again, but instead of feeling trapped, I was breaking the surface and finding freedom.

> Moses answered the people, "Do not be afraid. Stand
> firm and you will see the deliverance the LORD will
> bring you today. The Egyptians you see today you
> will never see again. The LORD will fight for you; you
> need only to be still." (Ex. 14:13–14 NIV)

This would not be my destruction, but my salvation. Jesus was reshuffling the deck of cards that was my life, and I was about to have a close and personal encounter with my Savior.

> But the eyes of the LORD are on those who fear him, on those whose hope is in his unfailing love, to deliver them from death and keep them alive in famine. We wait in hope for the LORD; he is our help and our shield. In him our hearts rejoice, for we trust in his holy name. May your unfailing love be with us, LORD, even as we put our hope in you. (Ps. 33:18–22 NIV)

Soon thereafter, Jesus would begin to intervene at times, allowing me to see the depth of His love more clearly. Within the fury of this whirlwind my life had become, the Lord brought sweet moments of comfort. Moments that made all the distress of what was happening melt away and seem not so important anymore. One such occasion involved the memory of my father. Due to my father's service in the Army, when he passed away, he was buried with military honors, and we requested a military footstone. We were told receipt of the footstone could take up to six months to arrive. With Memorial Day fast approaching, we were preparing the flowers for his grave and really had no expectation of seeing the stone yet. A few days prior to Memorial Day weekend, I was traveling out to the graveyard, and as I pulled into the entrance, a familiar song came on the radio. "There Will Be a Day"⁴ played softly on the radio, the same song playing the night we left the hospital. I knew it was not a coincidence; God is good. Then, walking up to the graveside, there it was—Dad's military footstone. God is great. Memorial Day somehow seemed complete and peaceful. Everything was finally in place at the site that honored my father's burial. When I visit his grave, it is not so much to remember what lies beneath the ground, for I know it is only an earthly vessel, but rather it is to reinforce the joy within me. The joy of knowing my father is now with his Father, and all the physical strains of this world have been removed from him. The joy of knowing I will see him again someday and will enjoy the sweetness of his smile and the quietness of his spirit.

Yes, after a long, hard fight, it was clear I would be a fatality in this battle for my career. Running out of resources and realizing that a door was closing, it came time to agree to disagree. A consent order is an agreement between the two parties that ends the legal proceeding, whether or not the two parties agree with any of the findings or actions that result. In this case, I was disagreeing with the findings, not accepting fault for any wrongdoing, but accepting the terms and conditions placed on me in order to move on. It was heartbreaking. Sixteen years I had walked in integrity, worked hard to raise the bar to a higher standard, and kept ethics at the forefront of my practice. With the stroke of a pen, all semblance of my career would be stained, overshadowed, veiled in question. All this because other people made a choice, other people decided to take matters into their own hands, other people thought they knew the whole story. The disillusion of what was happening could have eaten me alive, but somehow it just didn't seem as important as the events of the last few months. Career versus family is not a choice to me. Family will always be more important.

It was at this time that I was reminded by Jesus of the story of Elijah, a great prophet who was tested repeatedly by the Lord, thereby gaining insight and faith. The story of Elijah praying for rain (1 Kings 18:41–46 NKJV) teaches obedience, patience, and perseverance. Elijah makes a bold statement —rain is coming. Initially there are no clouds, no overcast, possibly just pure sunshine. Firmly, God has told him to proclaim it. Then he bows low to pray in the position of humility. He is not standing, not shouting, not boisterous in his request. Seven times he sends the servant to look. Back and forth the servant goes, and each time there is nothing. Nevertheless, Elijah sends him back until the last time when the servant, squinting his eyes, now sees a tiny cloud, a cloud no bigger than his own hand. In that moment, Elijah doesn't give up, he doesn't feel let down. He is confident. He instructs Ahab to go home. In the physical, Elijah looks foolish. His prayer looks ineffective and worthless. Surely, Ahab gave a good chuckle, but then it happens:

> And soon the sky was black with clouds. A heavy wind brought a terrific rainstorm, and Ahab left quickly for Jezreel. Then the LORD gave special strength to Elijah. He tucked his cloak into his belt and ran ahead of Ahab's chariot all the way to the entrance of Jezreel. (1 Kings 18:45–46 NLT)

No one is laughing now; they are leaving. They are bewildered and possibly irritated, but in truth, they are in awe of the God of Israel. Elijah is validated and vindicated; his faith has carried him.

Elijah's story is about timing. When we pray we don't always see results as soon as we desire. If we are obedient to what Christ tells us, humble in our request, and persistent in asking, God will answer. When we are in the Father's will, the answers will come. If we are not, He is gracious, provides strength, and calls us back. Somewhere along the way all of us step out of His will, sometimes innocently, sometimes purposely, needing to be called back. In His will is our purpose; in His will is our strength. A beautiful expression of our daily struggle, our faith journey, and our desired goal can be found in the song "Mountain of God":

> *Even though the journey's long,*
> *and I know the road is hard,*
> *well, the one who's gone before me,*
> *He will help me carry on.*

After all that I've been through,
now I realize the truth
that I must go through the valley,
to stand upon the mountain of God.[5]

I understand this walk is a faith walk meant to challenge and strengthen us to a point where we can stand in His promise. I was indeed experiencing some of the deepest valleys in life I had ever encountered. Though I was losing one battle, I was winning another, and the chains were falling off. I was determined I would wait upon the Lord for my little rain cloud, knowing that once it appeared, it would turn into a magnificent shower of blessings.

Paper and Ink

On my wall hangs paper and ink.
They tell the story of a road once traveled.
At one time, they defined me.
They would one day become a link in the chain that bound me.

But my Lord, my God, was not done.
He who began a good work in me would finish.
So He tore a page from the notebook,
and began the new blueprint.
It was uncomfortable; it was confusing.
It caused me to ask and to seek.
It made me look beyond the original paper and ink.

And I came to understand
His ways are higher than my ways.
His vision is far greater
than I had conceived.
Now when I look at my paper and ink,
they are confined to their frame,
but I am not.

For they were but stepping stones
to a path much wider.
Their significance cannot be more than my Lord's.
For who am I but the clay and He the potter.
So allow the Lord room to write out His plan.
But realize He requires a wide-open space.
And if you will allow Him to do His part,
He will write His will all over your heart.

CHAPTER 3

Life Redefined
~But This Isn't What I Picked Out~

Turn my eyes from worthless things, and give me
life through your word.
—Psalm 119:37 NLT

Once the consent order agreement was in place, I felt as if I was walking through no-man's-land. I was neither pessimistic nor optimistic; I was numb. For the first time in my life, there was no specific direction in which to head, no balance on which to fall back on. So many things either had to change or simply did change during the months that followed. Even so, life could have been dramatically different. I could have been someone who became extremely bitter about what I was going through. The strain of everything befalling us at once could have started feelings of discourse in my marriage and major doubt in my relationship with Jesus. I held on only by His grace and mercy.

Let everyone be subject to the governing authorities,
for there is no authority except that which God has
established. The authorities that exist have been

established by God. Consequently, whoever rebels against the authority is rebelling against what God has instituted, and those who do so will bring judgment on themselves. *For rulers hold no terror for those who do right, but for those who do wrong. Do you want to be free from fear of the one in authority? Then do what is right and you will be commended.* For the one in authority is God's servant for your good. But if you do wrong, be afraid, for rulers do not bear the sword for no reason. They are God's servants, agents of wrath to bring punishment on the wrongdoer. Therefore, it is necessary to submit to the authorities, not only because of possible punishment *but also as a matter of conscience.* (Rom. 13:1–5 NIV, italics mine)

The authority to which I was subject to was carrying out the duties of their jobs; however, their motivation concerning my case was clearly suspect. My experience is not the first case of self-motivated and unjustified use of power. It will not be the last. The Lord requires us to respect those in authority as it produces an overall order.

For God is not *the author* of confusion but of peace. (1 Cor. 14:33 NKJV)

Whether the motives of those in authority are right or wrong, God uses it all for His glory. Jesus is the perfect example of submission to authority, though He was completely innocent. As He was arrested, jailed, and even beaten, He was submissive to the process all for the glory of God's purpose. Jesus would not make a confession of guilt as there was none and only spoke in truth at key moments. In response to the false allegations, He was silent. He was not argumentative but calm through an extremely brutal process. His suffering had purpose. Jesus is our example for dealing with unsavory authority figures who abuse their power. Injustices will happen in this world; how they are faced will define them.

> Do not take revenge, my dear friends, but leave room for God's wrath, for it is written: "It is mine to avenge; I will repay," says the Lord. On the contrary: "If your enemy is hungry, feed him; if he is thirsty, give him something to drink. In doing this, you will heap burning coals on his head." Do not be overcome by evil, but overcome evil with good. (Rom. 12:19–21 NIV)

Moving forward was quite a challenge. For the better part of two years, we struggled financially, physically, and emotionally like no other time in our lives. We started this period of time by making numerous decisions regarding our current financial troubles. Months of attorney's fees piled onto everyday expenses minus a second income equaled huge debt. We learned to consolidate and cut unnecessary expenses, learned to budget our income, and let go of many pleasures we took for granted.

One of the most disheartening moments for me was selling my vehicle. I struggled materialistically with this one thing. It was not necessarily because of the type of vehicle it was, but because of what it symbolized to me. I made the purchase only because I felt proud of finishing nurse practitioner training and was, at the time, working in a reasonably successful practice. I saw it simply as a reward for the long, hard effort I put into becoming one of the best in my field. I wasn't selfish with it. I used it for my pleasure and the pleasure of others. I didn't wish it to be something between Jesus and me; I just wanted to enjoy life a little. When the time came to make the final decision to sell it, I remember asking the Lord, *Must I give up everything?* In my heart, He whispered, *I gave it all for you.* In the end, Jesus would teach me a valuable lesson about material possessions. Any possession in which one overextends oneself to get is not a reward but a stumbling block. We can't always see it for what it truly is until we have bruised our knees a few times from falling over it. Self-reward is fleeting; God's rewards are eternal.

> "Do not lay up for yourselves treasures on earth, where moth and rust destroy and where thieves break in and steal; but lay up for yourselves treasures in heaven, where neither moth nor rust destroys and where thieves do not break in and steal." (Matt. 6:19–20 NKJV)

In order to go where Jesus was leading, it was necessary to keep stripping away everything that was holding me back from the next level. Nothing was going to be left untouched, and it hurt. We first attempted to sell the vehicle at a local dealer; but we could not get what we needed to get out of the loan. Then we listed it and tried to sell it ourselves. After several months and a couple of deals that fell through, I headed back to the local dealer to try again. This time we were given enough not only to pay off the loan, but the excess took care of our current month end expenses. It was as if the Lord said, "Through your obedience, I will provide for all your needs." Suddenly, I began to realize that whatever I let go of was a gateway to whatever the Father was trying to get to me. This was the first hurdle in understanding God's provision.

> *In order to go where Jesus was leading, it was necessary to keep stripping away everything that was holding me back from the next level.*

At the lowest point in our financial drop, I remember having fifty dollars to our name once the bills were paid, the groceries bought, and the sacrifice of our tithe made to the church. Regardless, the provision never ran out. My husband and I committed to the process of tithing earlier in our spiritual walk. As our grasp of the exchange grew, we understood that the Lord is our creator, and He alone possesses everything within His creation. He gives us the ability to possess wealth (Deut. 8:18 NKJV), and He only requires a small portion of what we have in return (Gen. 14:20 NKJV). God does not need our money. He only desires the opportunity to show His ability to care for us.

> "Bring the whole tithe into the storehouse, that there may be food in my house. Test me in this," says the LORD Almighty, "and see if I will not throw open the floodgates of heaven and pour out so much blessing that there will not be room enough to store it." (Mal. 3:10 NIV)

Now, without any real financial security, faced with total uncertainty, would we continue to be faithful? Would we allow the God of the universe to provide for us? Would we allow ourselves to be totally reliant on Him for every need? Would we simply trust Him? This was a huge step in our walk.

No story of the Bible is more notable on the subject than the widow's mite (Mark 12:41–44, Luke 21:1–4 NKJV). This is a person we should long to be like in regard to her ability to trust God. In those days to be a widow was automatically equivalent to being poor. Possessionless, living off the kindness of family and strangers, nameless and powerless in the community, were widows. Bravely, she sought her God, against all outside pressures, she was obedient, and regardless of her circumstances, she gave all of herself. This is the true meaning of the exchange between God and man. He is not taking from us, but positioning us to receive.

Never had we needed Him to show up more than during this time and show up He would. People gave financial gifts to us, not just little gifts, but gifts of extravagant generosity. My husband experienced an increase in salary, we received various refunds, and tax breaks unexpectedly presented themselves. Over and over we were in awe at the way things fell into place, from good friends and family pouring out help in tangible ways to money just showing up unpredictably at precisely the right time. Please understand we didn't win the lottery. What we experienced was the Lord taking an interest in even the smallest need we had and meeting our needs without us. It was all Him, and there was no denying it. God honors the tithe, and He is faithful to care for those who willingly honor Him in this regard. Many people either disregard the spiritual law of the tithe or discount its power. I truly believe our financial recovery was solely connected to this faith challenge.

While we were learning to lean on the Lord financially, life would deliver another blow. This time I would be sucker punched as the battle crossed over to my husband's health and well-being. My husband and I met two months after I started nursing school. He has been there throughout my entire career. Throughout our twenty-one years of marriage, his calm, easy spirit has been a major source of strength, which I have drawn from many times. There is no doubt in my mind that Jesus placed him in my life. For my husband, a routine doctor's appointment would turn into a life-changing encounter. Lab work would lead to a biopsy, and the biopsy would end with the word *cancer*. I'm not sure there is anything more disturbing than facing such a diagnosis.

Never will I forget the feelings that washed over me. The emotions were mixed. Sadness at what was found and for what we could be facing, relief it had been caught so early (my husband was only forty-five at the time), and the reality of what might have been had it not been found until years down the road. Having initially been an oncology nurse, I was the support for many families dealing with this disease. Now my family was facing it. No one can conceive all the thoughts that race through your mind. Here was my best friend, the love of my life, and I was helpless to do anything. Right in that moment, I would have gladly taken his place. In that moment, everything changed. Talk about living on faith; it was absolutely all we had to hold on to.

Over the next few days to weeks, we let the news sink in and began the process of gathering as much information as possible. We were told we could take as much as a year to make a treatment decision because the cancer type was slow growing, and we had found it at an extremely early stage. Over the next several months, we would endure multiple tests and doctors' appointments in order to explore all the options. As time went on, surgery became the obvious answer. Recovery would prove more of a challenge, but together we faced it. In the end, my husband would be one of the lucky ones. His surgeon found an isolated tumor, and removal was successful. He would be declared cancer free postoperatively and each review of his lab work thereafter would reinforce that fact.

It is highly likely that in some cases this type of intense pressure and uncertainty could rip a marriage apart. Two huge life changes, loss of career and major disease could crush many a relationship. We would both cry and laugh together; we would share fears and concerns, and we would lean harder on Jesus than ever. We would find through His grace our marriage would become superglue strong. Life priorities were changing, and Jesus was with us each and every step.

> Love is patient, love is kind. It does not envy, it does
> not boast, it is not proud. It does not dishonor others,
> it is not self-seeking, it is not easily angered, it keeps
> no record of wrongs. Love does not delight in evil but
> rejoices with the truth. It always protects, always trusts,
> always hopes, always perseveres. (1 Cor. 13:4–7 NIV)

Although I wasn't headed back to practice, I was headed where Christ was leading. It was not what I was hoping for; it was simply the path He needed me to travel down. I became keenly aware that He was up to something, and if I could endure the process, where He was taking me was better than what I had planned.

> "My thoughts are nothing like your thoughts," says the LORD. "And my ways are far beyond anything you could imagine. For just as the heavens are higher than the earth, so my ways are higher than your ways and my thoughts higher than your thoughts." (Isa. 55:8–9 NLT)

The struggle to find work was disheartening. It was like falling into a sinkhole and struggling to get back to the surface. I did small jobs for a period of time. Slowly, I made the climb back; one job led into the opening of a bigger opportunity at the next job. I became stronger with each leap.

One of the last short-term jobs I had was teaching in the field of medical coding. The art of healing, for some time now, has been developing into an industry driven by the economics of our time. Healthcare being a billion-dollar industry requires a constant exchange of information and money to be viable. Your healthcare provider's care must be translated into a type of code, which is sent to insurance carriers for payment. Thus, the field of medical coding is exploding. For the better part of a year, I taught. I enjoyed using what I was gifted in to help others better their career. Having a clinical background was extremely useful because I could use my knowledge to educate these potential coders on what they were actually dealing with. Although not full-time work, it certainly was stabilizing.

I continued constantly to dig at where all this was leading. As I meditated on Scripture, little did I know that Jesus was working out an answer. A short while after beginning to look for full-time work again, I interviewed for a job custom-made for me. The employer was looking for someone in the nursing profession with coding experience to advise their multispecialty clinic on a day-to-day basis. There were no other applicants but me. It was *déjà vu*. Here the Lord was providing a job that only I could do. No words can describe the total awe of the moment. It was a major turning point in my life. Jesus wants so desperately to shower us with blessings. He delights in surprising us. He is real, my friend, and He is waiting for you. For all the heartache, for all the times of grief, for all the times of questioning and fear I went through, I am now grateful and extremely honored to have had such a close encounter with Him. To know I am important to the One who holds the world in His hands is humbling. Everyone can know Him! Will you allow Him to reveal Himself to you?

> Those who were my enemies without cause hunted me like a bird. They tried to end my life in a pit and threw stones at me; the waters closed over my head, and I thought I was about to perish. I called on your name, LORD, from the depths of the pit. You heard my plea: "Do not close your ears to my cry for relief." You came near when I called you, and you said, "Do not fear." You, Lord, took up my case; you redeemed my life. (Lam. 3:52–58 NIV)

I find it interesting that our human nature allows us to forgive ourselves more readily than we can believe our heavenly Father is not angry with us. We simply can't wrap our minds around the fact that we were created with a good purpose in mind. We deceive ourselves into believing somehow we can be good apart from Him. We substitute our standards in place of His because they seem more obtainable. What we are really attempting to do is do it ourselves, which certainly seems nobler. Beware, no one thrives in isolation. We yearn for relationships; we find strength in numbers. The void that persists is neither filled nor satisfied by the things we put in it. No one is exempt from the feeling of the void, but many people foolishly believe they will be the ones who conquer it. It exists because of Him. It was not created by a God angry with us, but one so in love with us that He built within us a place to woo us persistently. He doesn't stand in His heavens miles apart from us, but He lives on the outer rim of the void waiting for us to invite Him there. He does not desire us to live in darkness, but in the brilliance of His Light. He does not desire that we walk behind Him, but offers a place beside Him. We are constantly on His mind, even though He is not always on ours. Status is nothing to God; relationship is everything!

I would slowly, reluctantly, and tearfully release my status. Over the course of the last several years, I realized how wrapped up my self-image was in my status. For a period, the diplomas on my wall, the ones outlining my steps in life, defining my career, somehow took on a life of their own. They lured me into a false sense of security and safety. They flattered me into believing my success in life depended on them. They dulled my sense of hearing to the Father's call, and they shifted my focus onto earthly issues, not eternal ones. They pretended to be my life's work. So disenchanted by the current events surrounding me, I had to separate myself physically from them or risk drowning in their shadow. I removed them from the walls for a better part of two years, unable to bear their taunts and misleading promises. Broken, I could now be healed. Crushed, I could now truly begin again. No, this wasn't the work of an angry God, but a compassionate Savior saving me from myself. Life redefined, you bet. Thank goodness He holds an eraser.

One of my favorite stories in the Bible involves Jesus healing the woman with an issue of blood (Matt. 9:20–22, Mark 5:25–34, Luke 8:43–48 NKJV). We don't know her name; she is defined by her problem. She had suffered for years, most likely became an outcast as the community would have labeled her as unclean due to her disease. Although she had put her faith in numerous physicians, they had failed her. Her hope of a cure by worldly methods was gone. She had seemingly come to the end of the line. Having exhausted all the options, she was broken, her suffering was long, and still something burned inside her. She would hold out for a moment, a chance encounter with Jesus. She had no doubt heard of His healing power, planned her move, and then reached for the One and only One that could truly help her. Surrounded by hundreds, most likely thousands, she would push and stretch her way through this packed crowd until she reached Him.

> She had heard the reports concerning Jesus, and she came up behind Him in the throng and touched His garment, For she kept saying, If I only touch His garments, I shall be restored to health. And immediately her flow of blood was dried up at the source, and [suddenly] she felt in her body that she was healed of her [distressing] ailment. (Mark 5:27–29 AB)

In a moment, this woman defined by her condition, labeled due to disease, avoided due to her current status, would show tremendous faith. She would be healed, find peace, and experience love beyond imagination. She would be restored. After years of searching, no doubt her life was changed. She was no longer an outcast, and she recognized herself in a completely different light. As we enter into a true relationship with Him, Jesus requires us to throw off our worldly status and in exchange, He gives grace and mercy to all that seek it.

Over the course of two years, time would seem to stand still at moments. Time is the tool that Jesus uses to bring us to points of clarity. The quality of time shouldn't be measured by how quickly we gain insight, but by how deeply we allow the reshaping process to take hold of us. I can't tell you how long your time of refining will be, but the end result is always worth the process if you are open to it.

> While the Devil is a master manipulator, Jesus is the master of recreation.

Lord, You show Yourself in huge ways.
There is no problem too large or too small.
Your eyes are fixed upon those You love.
Your heart is loyal to those You call Your own.

We never see all that You do.
We never know all that You conceive.
We have only begun to uncover Your mysteries,
to know all You have put in motion.

When space and time and doubts no longer separate us,
will we then perceive only a part of all that You are?
Life is only a shadow, a mist we are passing through.
Time is only an illusion.
When all things are revealed, we will stand amazed,
overwhelmed by our lack of understanding,
our lack of wisdom.

How will we grasp all that You have for us?
Will You begin to teach us all over again?
What wonders do You have yet to show us,
what joys and surprises remain?

Thank you, Lord, for Your patience,
and thank you for Your grace.
May we work toward fulfillment of Your plan,
and to that end, bring love to a hurting world.

Chapter 4

The Road Less Traveled
~And All I Packed Was High Heel Shoes~

"You can enter God's Kingdom only through the
narrow gate. The highway to hell is broad, and its
gate is wide for the many who choose that way. But
the gateway to life is very narrow and the road is
difficult, and only a few ever find it."
—Matthew 7:13–14 (NLT)

The spiritual side of my journey would create a deep-seated need to explore all that Jesus is and all He has to offer. Christ was no longer a storybook character from my childhood, but a dynamic integral person leading my life. Throughout the events that unfolded, He would speak to me in many different ways and through many different avenues. There were days that I would sit outside under our carport and just listen for Him. Listening to nature, watching the wind move the earth's canvas, and just waiting for a word from the Lord was a regular occurrence. Meditating on His promises and the hope I had in Him was necessary to settle my restless mind.

One day as I sat pondering all that had happened, dreaming of a different future, a beautiful butterfly came and landed on my arm. It was as if he was sent to me and, in that moment, I felt the presence of the Holy Spirit. As I sat intrigued by this butterfly, I began to study this gentle creature. The first thing that caught my eye was his coloring. The top side of his wings was pitch black with light blue circular patterns; in contrast, the bottom side of his wings was black with orange circular patterns. To me, his coloring was a representation of our nature. The top side of his wings, cool, calming blue, represented our spirits, the place where Jesus connects with us through the Holy Spirit. The bottom side of his wings, fiery orange, represented our minds and souls. This part of us seems to be constantly in conflict mode fighting emotions, fighting doubt, and forever fighting against the Spirit. Secondly, I noticed his movements. As you watch a butterfly, even as he sits on top of the ground, a seemingly solid foundation, he is constantly moving his wings. Again, the comparison is striking. Aren't we like that, continuously struggling to quiet ourselves as one force inside us wars against the other? On the other hand, if we allow the Holy Spirit to connect and control our spirits, we can quiet the mind and soul. There were moments when his wings went down and stayed positioned that way. Full expansion of his wings means complete coverage of his body. I felt the Lord say, "Keep your wings down, quiet yourself, and let My spirit cover you."

> So he said to me, "This is the word of the LORD to Zerubbabel: 'Not by might nor by power, but by my Spirit,' says the LORD Almighty." (Zech. 4:6 NIV)

Since this encounter, I have learned when to keep my wings down.

I have also felt a connection to another character of the Bible—Joseph. No character of the Bible knows more about denied justice than Joseph. Three times he was denied justice.

He experienced rejection at the hands of his brothers, who in a jealous rage contemplated even murdering him, but opted to sell him into slavery.

> "Here comes that dreamer!" they said to each other. "Come now, let's kill him and throw him into one of these cisterns and say that a ferocious animal devoured him. Then we'll see what comes of his dreams." When Reuben heard this, he tried to rescue him from their hands. "Let's not take his life," he said. "Don't shed any blood. Throw him into this cistern here in the wilderness, but don't lay a hand on him." Reuben said this to rescue him from them and take him back to his father ... Judah said to his brothers, "What will we gain if we kill our brother and cover up his blood? Come, let's sell him to the Ishmaelites and not lay our hands on him; after all, he is our brother, our own flesh and blood." His brothers agreed. (Gen. 37:19–22, 26–27 NIV)

He experienced the consequences of false allegations when Potiphar's wife accused him of rape, a crime he did not commit.

> One day he went into the house to attend to his duties, and none of the household servants was inside. She caught him by his cloak and said, "Come to bed with me!" But he left his cloak in her hand and ran out of the house. When she saw that he had left his cloak in her hand and had run out of the house, she called her household servants. "Look," she said to them, "this Hebrew has been brought to us to make sport of us! He came in here to sleep with me, but I screamed. When he heard me scream for help, he left his cloak beside me and ran out of the house." (Gen. 39:11–15 NIV)

He experienced isolation when the Pharaoh's cupbearer and baker abandoned him in jail, even after interpreting their dreams for them.

> Now the third day was Pharaoh's birthday, and he gave a feast for all his officials. He lifted up the heads of the chief cupbearer and the chief baker in the presence of his officials: He restored the chief cupbearer to his position, so that he once again put the cup into Pharaoh's hand— but he impaled the chief baker, just as Joseph had said to them in his interpretation. The chief cupbearer, however, did not remember Joseph; he forgot him. (Gen. 40:20–23 NIV)

In spite of everything, we know from Scripture that the Lord was with him. When you are in line for something from God, opposition will come. Jesus uses this to mold and shape you, to prepare you for your true purpose in life. Our reactions to our circumstances, but more importantly, our reactions to our Savior, regardless of the circumstances, will determine the order of our steps. In the book of Psalms, the Lord's timing concerning Joseph is explained.

> *Our reactions to our circumstances, but more importantly, our reactions to our Savior, regardless of the circumstances, will determine the order of our steps.*

> He called down famine on the land and destroyed all their supplies of food; and he sent a man before them—Joseph, sold as a slave. They bruised his feet with shackles, his neck was put in irons, *till*

what he foretold came to pass, till the word of the LORD proved him true. The king sent and released him, the ruler of peoples set him free. He made him master of his household, ruler over all he possessed, to instruct his princes as he pleased and teach his elders wisdom. (Ps. 105:16–22 NIV, italics mine)

I so relate to the story of Joseph. There are so many common factors: having a dream, feeling the grip of pride, being cast out and stripped of status, being falsely accused, having to rebuild from the ground up, and having to be consistent in my faith in order to survive it all. Ironically, the story of Joseph, like many others, is not about Joseph. It is about God's will and His ability to accomplish that will in spite of humanity. It's about God wanting to use every single human being for His glory, but having to search and find those who will trust Him. It's about a God who, through Jesus, can carry you, push you, and deliver you into a destiny bigger than you can conceive.

Whoever dwells in the shelter of the Most High will rest in the shadow of the Almighty. I will say of the LORD, "He is my refuge and my fortress, my God, in whom I trust." ... "Because he loves me," says the LORD, "I will rescue him; I will protect him, for he acknowledges my name. He will call on me, and I will answer him; I will be with him in trouble, I will deliver him and honor him. With long life I will satisfy him and show him my salvation." (Ps. 91:1–2, 14–16 NIV)

Serious hope and faith allows us to reengage the Father through our Savior, and we can reconnect with Jesus no matter how life gets derailed. Are we expecting Jesus to follow us, or are we willing to follow Jesus?

> In order for us to reestablish our relationship with
> Jesus, we have to have the humility to admit we
> walked away.—Perry Noble[1]

Day after day, week after week, I clung to the safety of my church family and listened intently for a word from the Lord. He would speak powerful words into my life through the pastors of my church. Repeatedly, I would hear the Word spoken with unbreakable truths that changed my life. During one particular sermon series titled *One Prayer,* God would let me know His plans would go forth regardless of the circumstances; they are simply unstoppable.

> Your mistakes won't stop His plans.
> Others' malice won't stop His plans.
> Satan's attacks won't stop His plans.[2]

At the same time, there are specific plans He holds for us as individuals. We can have hope that when we participate in life with Jesus, those plans will be realized.

> For we are God's masterpiece. He has created us
> anew in Christ Jesus, so we can do the good things
> he planned for us long ago. (Eph. 2:10 NLT)

> Most of us underestimate what God wants to
> accomplish in us and through us. I'm not sure if we
> underestimate ourselves, or we underestimate who
> God is. God is big; God is amazing; God is huge; God
> is powerful. Do you really think an amazing, powerful
> God is going to choose you and give you a plan for
> your life that is a ho-hum, anybody could do it kind of
> plan?—Jamey Stuart[3]

A life fully committed to the Father will never be average! There will be ups and downs as you find your way. Indeed, there were times when I was certain I had reached my limits, and that I couldn't express to Jesus anymore how much I wanted out of my situation.

> "And now my life seeps away. Depression haunts my days. At night my bones are filled with pain, which gnaws at me relentlessly." (Job 30:16–17 NLT)

When those times came, He would keep filling me up with His love and grace.

During a women's conference at church, I found myself mesmerized by the Spirit. I drank in long and deep the words spoken at that conference. The resounding theme was the Lord's faithfulness to those that keep their eyes locked on Him. The story of Caleb was used to demonstrate this principle. Caleb was one of twelve men sent to explore the Promised Land prior to the Israelites possessing it (Num. 13 NKJV). He alone would stand with Joshua in believing that Israel would succeed in taking the land regardless of the current inhabitants. God in turn remembered him.

> "But my servant Caleb—this is a different story. He has a different spirit; he follows me passionately. I'll bring him into the land that he scouted and his children will inherit it." (Num. 14:24 MSG)

Even forty-five years later, Caleb is still praising his God and holding on to the promise given to him so long ago, and God would deliver.

> "Now then, just as the LORD promised, he has kept me alive for forty-five years since the time he said this

> to Moses, while Israel moved about in the wilderness.
> So here I am today, eighty-five years old! I am still as
> strong today as the day Moses sent me out; I'm just
> as vigorous to go out to battle now as I was then.
> Now give me this hill country that the LORD promised
> me that day." ... Then Joshua blessed Caleb son of
> Jephunneh and gave him Hebron as his inheritance.
> (Josh. 14:10–13 NIV)

No matter how long it takes, keep praising Him. God will deliver.

During a time of praise and worship, a time given to reach for God, I found myself doing something I had never done before. I cried out to the Lord that day like no time in my life. I came up front to the place of meditation, and I lifted my hands and my face to heaven. I let the tears flow, and when they came, I could not control the flood that washed over me. In a room full of people, I was no longer going to be just part of the crowd. I was going to reach God. I was all in. I was not leaving that spot on the carpet until He understood my pain, my desperation, my need. Sitting there, I knew that God was not surprised by me, but He was only waiting for me to ask, to want, to need Him that much. There was no going back after that day. I became free. Free to seek my Father in heaven to a depth that inspired me. No longer was I a captive of insecurity and fear, no longer just a person in the room, but a child of the King.

Jesus continued to work on my heart. He would send me another message that became an anthem to my soul. I had strengthened; I was healing, and now I just needed a healthy dose of courage. It would come during the sermon series *Sun Stand Still*. The series, based on the original book titled as such, would be for me a total revelation. Suddenly, many events of the past few years started making sense. However, the rawness of the hurt was still there; it was less, but still there, just enough to keep the full excitement of what I was hearing at bay. Over time, the hurt would pass, and my mind would open to all the possibilities life had to offer.

In the book *Sun Stand Still,*[4] Joshua is the person of interest. Joshua would lead the Israelites into the Promised Land after the death of Moses. He would prove to be a mighty leader and a ferocious warrior. Before Israel could call the land home, there were many battles to be fought. Joshua would cry out to God in the midst of the most heated battle and ask a seemingly impossible favor of the Lord.

> On the day the LORD gave the Amorites over to Israel, Joshua said to the LORD in the presence of Israel:
>
> "Sun, stand still over Gibeon, and you, moon, over the Valley of Aijalon."
>
> So the sun stood still, and the moon stopped, till the nation avenged itself on its enemies, as it is written in the Book of Jashar. The sun stopped in the middle of the sky and delayed going down about a full day. There has never been a day like it before or since, a day when the LORD listened to a human being. Surely the LORD was fighting for Israel! (Josh. 10:12–14 NIV)

The question remains, are we brave enough to call out to our God in the midst of our battles and make bold, spectacular requests relaying our conviction that He alone is God *and* that He can do anything?

So many things flooded my spirit during this time, and my perspective shifted. One single thought would completely thrill me.

> You might be thinking you're unimpressive and unqualified. That's good. God performs the most impressive feats through the most unimpressive people. God likes to wet the wood before he sets

it on fire. That way, everybody knows who made it
burn.—Steve Furtick[5]

That statement, based on 1 Kings 18:33–38 (NKJV), set off
something inside me. I read and reread this story. Elijah is once
again in front of the people of Israel. He has restored the altar
and prepared a sacrifice, but then he does something unusual.
He asks for water to be poured over the altar and the sacrifice
not once but three times. Then he calls upon the Lord to perform
a miracle, and God responds. Everything is consumed by fire
from heaven; there is nothing left but ashes. There is little doubt
who performed this feat. This scene resounded with me—I was
the wood! I wasn't damp; I wasn't wet; I was soaked! Jesus
was in the middle of a setup, and I was the object of it. When
we become less, He becomes more so that when the plan is
revealed, God is glorified.

So I prayed:

Father God, my steps are not my own. You order my steps;
You know the plans You have for me, good not evil. I know I
need more of the Word, so open my eyes to things I overlook
so I can see. Guide me down the path You are leading. I no
longer want anything in me to resist. For Your glory and Your
glory alone, finish my testimony in a way only You can, so it is
plain for all to see I am just a servant of Jesus, the One, the
true great King. In Christ's name, I pray. Amen.

Listening to the *Sun Stand Still* series[6] gave me the courage
to speak out about what the Lord was doing in my life. I may
have been in a time of delay, but I was not forgotten. Jesus was
working. Throughout this entire course of time, He was slowly
removing obstacles that would hinder me from seeking Him and
replacing them with things that allowed a clearer vision for my life.

When you go through deep waters, I will be with you.
When you go through rivers of difficulty, you will not

drown. When you walk through the fire of oppression, you will not be burned up; the flames will not consume you. For I am the LORD, your God, the Holy One of Israel, your Savior ... *But forget all that—it is nothing compared to what I am going to do. For I am about to do something new. See, I have already begun! Do you not see it?* I will make a pathway through the wilderness. I will create rivers in the dry wasteland. (Isa. 43:2–3, 18–19 NLT, italics mine)

Can you say to Jesus, "I know You are great; I know You are awesome. You can handle my issues, questions, and doubts. In fact, You can handle all of me at the same time You handle everything else in the world! It is no match for You. Here I am, use me."

Slowly, over time, I would feel a little stronger, and I would heal. More importantly, I would be different. Jesus would give me a little more direction, a little more hope, and all the while, a furious faith was growing. I began truly to understand that my Creator knew me. He knew when to give me more and when to hold back.

"Be still, and know that I am God!" (Psalm 46:10 NLT)

Then the Lord honored me with something I was not expecting. Three years after the start of such a tumultuous time, I went to a medical conference related to pain management. Although I was not currently practicing, I continued to follow the present educational themes of the specialty out of genuine interest. I had no idea the conference was another piece to my overall healing. During my time at the conference, I interacted with various national leaders in pain management. When I felt led, I would share my story with them. One particular speaker took a real interest in my story and asked if I could be contacted later.

That single conversation would lead to an invitation to speak at the next national pain conference. It was an unexpected honor. Here were peers within the pain management community, who had written numerous articles and even textbooks, asking me to share the stage with them and tell about my experience. Never would I have dreamed of that happening. When the time came, I was flown out to the beautiful West Coast. There this no-named girl from the East Coast would be treated once again like a well-rounded, educated professional. My peers in the specialty would welcome me in as one of their own. There was no shame or guilt to feel for having fallen from grace. It was like being home after a long journey. After my presentation, there was true understanding of my struggle, validation of my skills and knowledge, but most importantly, there was true kindness shown by those around me. They will never know how much their respect and support meant. It was indeed a special moment. I thank the Lord for giving me such an opportunity to release the past and to know I am not alone. It was one of the most touching moments of my life.

> Then Hannah prayed: "My heart rejoices in the LORD! The LORD has made me strong. Now I have an answer for my enemies; I rejoice because you rescued me. No one is holy like the LORD! There is no one besides you; there is no Rock like our God." "Stop acting so proud and haughty! Don't speak with such arrogance! For the LORD is a God who knows what you have done; he will judge your actions." ... "He will protect his faithful ones, but the wicked will disappear in darkness. No one will succeed by strength alone." (1 Sam. 2:1-3, 9 NLT)

This prayer by Hannah, wife of Elkana, was prayed after the birth of a son for whom she had waited for quite some time.

Prior to his birth, she was considered barren and was ridiculed by Elkana's other wife who had children. The Bible states she had previously prayed in deep anguish, crying bitterly. Now she would pray with great joy. The emotions of both prayers describe well the emotions I would go through during this awakening of my spirit. I knew without a doubt my prayers were reaching God, and there was great comfort in that alone.

Life is distracting; you have to push it away.
Like drawing back the curtains, even on a long rainy day.
If you can get through it, the sun will come back out.
Because it has been there all along,
you just thought it was blotted out.

When you feel like it will never end, just hold on; it never lasts.
It will make you stronger.
It will make you bolder.
It will make you more determined if you let it do the work.

If you cry out, He will hear you.
If you reach out, He will catch you.
If you believe, He will remove the doubt.
If you pray, He will hear.
If you draw close, He draws closer.
If you ask, He will respond.

The impossible is possible.
The unseen is visible.
The unheard is audible.
The untouchable is in reach.
The lost are found.
The broken are healed.

CHAPTER 5

Life, His Way
~When I Grow Up~

Look to the LORD and his strength; seek his face always.
—Psalm 105:4 (NIV)

Another area Jesus would work on in my life is serving God's purposes right here and right now. As events would progress, change, and then start to settle, the challenge would be to fill all those moments in between with positive service. So many times when tragedy befalls us, our first impulse is to collapse within ourselves. During these times, the Devil has the best opportunity to discourage us and make our walk ineffective. Serving the Master by serving others is by far the greatest defense we have available next to prayer. There were certainly times I would become immobile, but I pushed to minimize them. At each level of obedience, Jesus would bring a higher level of service and responsibility.

> *Serving the Master by serving others is by far the greatest defense we have available next to prayer.*

I have mentioned that one area in which my husband and I have served is as small group leaders. As we continued to help in this area, I was also privileged to work as a small group team leader. In this role I would serve, encourage, and pray for other small group leaders during the small group semester. During some of the time I was out of work, I volunteered in the church office. Once a week, I would stuff the worship folders, or bulletins as some call them. Just this simple task would allow people entering our church, perhaps for the first time, a chance to discover what the church had to offer them. It was exciting to see the number of worship folders increase slowly and steadily as more people attended. For a long period of time, I worked at our resource center on Sundays. This service area of our welcome center provides information for upcoming events, copies of the service, and books to read. Of late, I have had the awesome responsibility to pray with people at the end of our evening service. Nothing is more exciting and humbling than to pray for others, interceding for them the way Jesus does for us.

Volunteering at church in various areas would ground me in serving others. I took these duties as seriously as any job I had been paid to do. Jesus needs people who are willing to start on the ground floor and work their way up to levels of service uniquely designed for them. No one should expect to step into the high-level positions He offers without first surrendering to His mentorship. We do not walk into any job without having an orientation or some training. You can't understand the mission or the goals of the company's owner without knowing or implementing them into your daily work. If you are bold enough to ask Jesus to use you, expect Him to train you. Expect molding and direction that challenges you, stretches you, and causes you to cry out. Are you ready for this promotion? How bad do you want it? I caution you, He hears the desires of our hearts. Don't put it out there if you don't mean it.

Somewhere in my search to understand all that was happening, I came across the story of Jabez and the prayer he boldly prayed. So bold was this request that he got a two-verse mention in the Bible.

> Now Jabez was more honorable than his brothers, and his mother called his name Jabez, saying, "Because I bore *him* in pain." And Jabez called on the God of Israel saying, "Oh, that You would bless me indeed, and enlarge my territory, that Your hand would be with me, and that You would keep *me* from evil, that I may not cause pain!" So God granted him what he requested. (1 Chron. 4:9–10 NKJV)

The prayer has been interpreted by many as a cry from Jabez for the Lord to use him for big things. There are four themes that have been taken from this prayer: a request for supernatural favor, a request to increase the impact one makes, admitted dependence on God to accomplish the impossible, and a request of protection. Boldness, inspiration, and life change are the thoughts contained in this small section of Scripture. And God's reply, He granted him what he requested!

I placed the Jabez prayer over the mirror in my bathroom. I read those words over and over every day. I read them sometimes in passing, but didn't commit to them. I was still secretly hoping that things would turn around. Other times I read those words with intention regardless of whether I got what I wanted or not. I read those words until I could be committed to what He was going to do, until my selfish wants subsided, until I believed His path was better than the one I attempted to create. It challenged me.

It made me uncomfortable.

It made me wonder.

It made me open up.

It made me determined to see this through.

The nature of thinking we know best has to be broken before He can truly work. I would either believe Jesus or live a life wondering what could have been. I would not settle for the latter. I felt it deep in my soul; He had not brought me to this place to die. Everything screamed within me, there is more to come.

> "God blesses those who are poor and realize their
> need for him, for the Kingdom of Heaven is theirs."
> (Matt. 5:3 NLT)

I was about to be used in ways I had not contemplated before, in a place I had never thought of before. Our church began planning its first out of country missions trip at the height of my struggles. I didn't have to think twice about whether to go or not. I was ready from the first discussion. Destination—Nicaragua.

Nicaragua is a country that has been broken by revolts and revolutions. It is a country full of people seeking some form of hope and happiness, surrounded by spiritual darkness. A country so poverty stricken that everyday survival is a miracle itself. As an American, I don't think you can ever really be prepared to go to a country such as this one. To see people who are without any real modern comforts is a stark contrast to our society. To know that families with four to eight members may live in a small home containing three or four rooms separated by nothing more than a sheet gives a whole new meaning to tight quarters. To see a child walk for quite a distance, either by himself or with even younger siblings in tow, cup and bowl in their hands, just to receive a meal, is gripping. To live in a country with an 85 to 90 percent unemployment rate compared to our mere 7 to 8 percent unemployment rate is unthinkable.

Still, while spending time there, Jesus allowed me to see a different side. There, underneath all the need, is a beautiful culture of people who have the same basic needs as us; love, relationship, and a need for a Savior. They contain a deep sense of family.

They, in spite of all their struggles, are not only a gracious people, but also a satisfied, loving people as well. They are not bitter; they are practical. They are not frozen; they just keep moving.

Here is a country ahead of a few places around the world, but still so far behind the more developed areas, and the Lord is with them. He has not forgotten them. Spiritual leaders are rising up and creating a foothold for the Gospels. Children who would go hungry are being fed and clothed. They are being taught skills that can take them out of their circumstances. People, able to help this effort, are being reached, and lifelines of both financial and spiritual aid are coming into this place. It is a rebuilding of the physical, emotional, mental, and spiritual nature, in that order. It is all filtered through the local church. It runs on faith, and it is a complete orchestration by almighty God.

> "Therefore I tell you, do not worry about your life, what you will eat or drink; or about your body, what you will wear. Is not life more than food, and the body more than clothes? Look at the birds of the air; they do not sow or reap or store away in barns, and yet your heavenly Father feeds them. Are you not much more valuable than they? Can any one of you by worrying add a single hour to your life?" "And why do you worry about clothes? See how the flowers of the field grow. They do not labor or spin. Yet I tell you that not even Solomon in all his splendor was dressed like one of these. If that is how God clothes the grass of the field, which is here today and tomorrow is thrown into the fire, will he not much more clothe you—you of little faith?" (Matt. 6:25–30 NIV)

Since the first trip down, I have thought to myself how small my troubles over the last few years seem. If they can be satisfied with what little they have, could I not be happy with what I had left? If the Lord could take care of such a group of people and supply their most basic needs, can He not care for me?

This became my meeting ground with Christ. This became the place where I would wrestle with everything that had happened and yet know my life continued to have purpose. Now broken and spiritually sensitive to His whisperings, our mission here on earth was revealed in vivid reality. Suddenly, in this foreign place surrounded by the extremes of happiness and sadness, I found myself for the first time seeing the entire world the way He sees it. Jesus doesn't see us in our richness or poorness.

Jesus doesn't see us in good times or bad.

Jesus doesn't see us by culture, race, or sex.

He only sees us, and *nothing* keeps us hidden.

> Nothing in all creation is hidden from God. Everything is naked and exposed before his eyes, and he is the one to whom we are accountable. (Heb. 4:13 NLT)

In this place, I would meet my Savior in a way I had never truly let myself experience Him, as my one true source of happiness and purpose. Stripped of everything that was blinding me, now I could see and most importantly; I could be used.

> You will seek me and find me when you seek me with all your heart. (Jer. 29:13 NIV)

Nicaragua, for me, is one of the most powerful demonstrations of Christ's love and ultimate control I have ever experienced. Many notable things have occurred during my travels there, but I want to share an experience I had the very first trip. It is a lesson in the small role we play and the huge gap that Jesus readily fills.

As we started planning that initial trip, the Lord planted a seed in my heart to speak to the young girls there concerning their female health. It was definitely of the Lord, as this has never been my background or focus in nursing, but something stirred inside me to fill this need. Having no knowledge about this area of the world and not able to speak the language, I wondered how in the world I would pull this off. God is good.

In my mind, I thought I'd speak to about thirty girls from the orphanage, and it would be a nice afternoon. God had bigger plans! If you let God use you, He will provide. For me, the needs were knowledge, opportunity, and assistance. Not long after arriving in Nicaragua, I discovered I had a counterpart there, an American nurse who had dedicated the last several years of her life to this area of the country and to the orphanage. Through this connection, the Lord provided knowledge. From her time spent there, I would learn what the cultural issues were, what the girls needed to hear, and what they had been experiencing. Next, the Lord provided opportunity. I didn't speak once, but four times. I spoke once a day for four days with almost fifty girls in each class. By the end of the week, I had spoken to around two hundred girls! The sweet thing was, the Lord even provided assistance, because on our team was a biology teacher who came with me to help teach the class and answer questions. It was a perfect fit.

While teaching them the importance of female health, we spoke love to them. We told them God had a plan for each of them, which may or may not include children. We told them the Lord created man and woman to have stable relationships in which to bring children into the world. Lastly, we told them it was good to have dreams and to want those dreams that He planted in their hearts. It is my greatest desire to see them grow up and become the women He created them to be. Please pray for the young women of Nicaragua.

Since then, I go to Nicaragua yearly. I watch as the hands of Jesus change the small town we visit through the hearts and souls of those living there. I watch children who have been taken in and cared for, that were once hungry and/or abused, beginning to thrive. They are growing physically, but more importantly, they are growing spiritually. They know there is a Father in heaven that watches over them, a Savior who loves them, and people who are committed to their well-being surrounding them. I watch a pastor and his wife, whose hearts are broken for their community and their country, give of themselves daily in the most practical ways. I have watched the local feeding center take in children from the city, desperate for food, and transform their lives one meal at a time. I am witnessing the birth of a new generation of believers who will become the salvation of their country. I am convinced they will one day win Nicaragua for the Lord.

> For the foolishness of God is wiser than human wisdom, and the weakness of God is stronger than human strength. Brothers and sisters, think of what you were when you were called. Not many of you were wise by human standards; not many were influential; not many were of noble birth. But God chose the foolish things of the world to shame the wise; God chose the weak things of the world to shame the strong. God chose the lowly things of this world and the despised things—and the things that are not—to nullify the things that are, so that no one may boast before him. (1 Cor. 1:25–29 NIV)

When we start to see this life as more than an opportunity for us to prosper, we start to understand our true purposes. We are meant to be reflectors of light in a dimly lit world. We are meant to love and to serve others. I watch people all the time who believe if they can make a few more dollars in their check, drive a nicer car, live in a bigger house, or get a promotion at work, life would be better, and they would be happy. Even Solomon states it is all vanity.

> I said to myself, "Come on, let's try pleasure. Let's look for the 'good things' in life." But I found that this, too, was meaningless. (Eccl. 2:1 NLT)

One cannot be encircled by such displays of mercy and grace, as in Nicaragua, and not be radically changed. There, among the mild background noise of busy streets, is a calm, quiet, untouched place. The busyness of America fades, and I hear only the footsteps of Christ. Jesus shows Himself everywhere, and although He is present in America, He is palpable in Nicaragua.

> But Jesus called them together and said, "You know that the rulers in this world lord it over their people, and officials flaunt their authority over those under them. But among you it will be different. Whoever wants to be a leader among you must be your servant, and whoever wants to be first among you must become your slave. For even the Son of Man came not to be served but to serve others and to give his life as a ransom for many." (Matt. 20:25–28 NLT)

Jesus spoke clearly about being a servant. Humbly, He came into this world to demonstrate the attitudes and behaviors we are to mimic. Throughout His ministry, He allowed Himself to be used, and not once did He request or require notoriety. In order to truly serve those around us, we must be willing to forego the accolades of others. True service does not factor recognition into the equation.

We prove ourselves by our purity, our understanding, our patience, our kindness, by the Holy Spirit within us, and by our sincere love ... Our hearts ache, but we always have joy. We are poor, but we give spiritual riches to others. We own nothing, and yet we have everything.
—2 Corinthians 6:6, 10 (NLT)

CHAPTER 6

Are We There Yet?
~Enough Said~

Search me, O God, and know my heart; test me
and know my anxious thoughts. Point out anything
in me that offends you, and lead me along the path
of everlasting life.
—Psalm 139:23–24 (NLT)

During any journey that lasts an extended period of time, those famous four words are bound to come up: Are we there yet? However, when our only goal is to reach the end, we have already given up on the overall purpose of why we left in the first place. Our journey through life is birthed out of hope and expectations. Instinctively, we know there will be some surprises along the way. So where do we get off track? In a word—knowledge.

I challenge you, whether you are a new Christian or a longtime Christian still trying to identify your purpose in life, to dive into God's Word. If the salvation message is the only message you hear, move on. If the only type of prosperity message you hear has you knee-deep in the acquisition of material possessions, run.

If the only time Jesus hears from you is when things are wrong, change your focus. If you feel you have put it all on the line for Christ, but you have not seen anything happen yet, keep pushing.

> Stagnation is the true enemy of our soul. If we are not growing spiritually, we have widened the playing field for the Devil. He will not hesitate to make a move when he sees an opening.

For me, as the days turned into weeks, weeks turned into months, and months turned into years, I asked the question, "How long will this last?" Nevertheless, with each passing day, my peace only grew.

> You will keep in perfect peace those whose minds are steadfast, because they trust in you. Trust in the LORD forever, for the LORD, the LORD himself, is the Rock eternal. (Isa. 26:3–4 NIV)

I stood firm in my faith that God, through Jesus, controls my life.

> For the LORD is our judge, the LORD is our lawgiver, the LORD is our king; it is he who will save us. (Isa. 33:22 NIV)

I fully trusted in the promises of my Savior.

> "The grass withers and the flowers fall, but the word of our God endures forever." (Isa. 40:8 NIV)

And I knew the mission ahead of me.

> The Spirit of the Sovereign LORD is on me, because the LORD has anointed me to proclaim good news to

the poor. He has sent me to bind up the brokenhearted, to proclaim freedom for the captives and release from darkness for the prisoners, to proclaim the year of the LORD's favor and the day of vengeance of our God, to comfort all who mourn, and provide for those who grieve in Zion—to bestow on them a crown of beauty instead of ashes, the oil of joy instead of mourning, and a garment of praise instead of a spirit of despair. They will be called oaks of righteousness, a planting of the LORD for the display of his splendor. (Isa. 61:1–3 NIV)

Without a personal walk with Jesus, I could not have gained this footing any other way. After so much anguish and heartache, after the recovery and the healing, the question really worth asking was, "Am I the person Chirst needs me to be?"

Then I realized that my heart was bitter, and I was all torn up inside. I was so foolish and ignorant—I must have seemed like a senseless animal to you. Yet I still belong to you; you hold my right hand. You guide me with your counsel, leading me to a glorious destiny. Whom have I in heaven but you? I desire you more than anything on earth. My health may fail, and my spirit may grow weak, but God remains the strength of my heart; he is mine forever. (Ps. 73:21–26 NLT)

In honesty, this truth remains—we are all works in progress. I can't compare myself to Jesus. He is too marvelous and too wonderful. No doubt, Christ is the standard we strive for, but until the day He walks among us again, we will not reach that ultimate goal. So what do we do in the meantime? For myself, I look to Paul, and I hope that my life mimics his zeal and great passion in following our Lord. The life of the apostle Paul both challenges and inspires. I would say since so much of his life is revealed in the Bible it bears review.

> *In honesty, this truth remains—*
> *we are all works in progress.*

Paul's beginnings carry a dark undertone. As we read through the book of Acts about Paul (known initially as Saul), he is far from God. He is religious but not saved. His faith is in the law, not the Lord, and he is committing heinous crimes against those called Christians. Amazingly, Chirst in His infinite love meets Paul where he is and starts a change in him that will play out page after page in the New Testament. The change in Paul is radical. Here is someone who takes in the Lord's promises and immediately gets to work. He doesn't allow his past to define him, but rather he uses it as a backdrop to highlight the vast change that his Savior has made in his life. He is bold; he is fearless; he is sold out for the One who gave it all.

What is the secret to Paul's success? Underneath it all, he was humble, he was grateful, and he was totally reliant on Jesus' gift of mercy and grace. His sensitivity to the various cultures he encountered is desirable. His hunger to cover more and more ground is insatiable. His heart to have everyone hear the Gospels is unmatched. He could not be silenced nor could he be contained. His joy was contagious; his peace was sought after. What he endured was unimaginable, yet he was more than resilient. He was relentless. Not a moment could be spared if it took away from the spreading of the Gospels. There was no one too far gone for Paul to reach out to and share this message of love. He was selfless, and he was unashamed!

> For I am not ashamed of this Good News about Christ.
> It is the power of God at work, saving everyone who
> believes—the Jew first and also the Gentile. (Rom.
> 1:16 NLT)

These are the powerful things we remember about Paul. We do not think of the times he was delayed, the times he was turned away, the times he was shut down. Why should we? Paul didn't. There was no looking back. His focus was always forward to the next time he could minister. He was determined to accomplish everything Christ needed him to do. He used even the times of silence he experienced as a time to seek guidance and direction in his next assignment. His determination allowed him to push beyond the most constraining physical and emotional roadblocks he encountered.

Paul's commitment to the Gospels, his discipline in self-improvement, and his love of fellow man has left us with some of the most detailed and insightful messages on how to live the Christian life.

Examples of Paul's Writings

> We can rejoice, too, when we run into problems
> and trials, for we know that they help us develop
> endurance. And endurance develops strength of
> character, and character strengthens our confident
> hope of salvation. And this hope will not lead to
> disappointment. For we know how dearly God loves
> us, because he has given us the Holy Spirit to fill our
> hearts with his love. (Rom. 5:3–5 NLT)

Paul gives us the building blocks that God uses to strengthen us. Each one is another layer to a solid foundation. Each time we go through the process, we become a little more fortified. Through it all, we are reminded of God's love for us.

> Three things will last forever—faith, hope, and love—
> and the greatest of these is love. (1 Cor. 13:13 NLT)

Paul points out that the greatest possession we have is love. Without it, we are empty, never satisfied, and adrift in an unforgiving world.

> Don't be misled—you cannot mock the justice of God. You will always harvest what you plant. Those who live only to satisfy their own sinful nature will harvest decay and death from that sinful nature. But those who live to please the Spirit will harvest everlasting life from the Spirit. So let's not get tired of doing what is good. At just the right time we will reap a harvest of blessing if we don't give up. (Gal. 6:7–9 NLT)

Paul reminds us of the law of sowing and reaping, and he encourages us that the time of reward is only one blessing away.

> And now, dear brothers and sisters, one final thing. Fix your thoughts on what is true, and honorable, and right, and pure, and lovely, and admirable. Think about things that are excellent and worthy of praise. Keep putting into practice all you learned and received from me—everything you heard from me and saw me doing. Then the God of peace will be with you. (Phil. 4: 8–9 NLT)

Paul instructs us on how to keep a pleasing attitude. He is well aware that this is not easily done, so he tells us to fix our thoughts. We can control what we think, but it takes effort.

> Live wisely among those who are not believers,
> and make the most of every opportunity. Let your
> conversation be gracious and attractive so that you will
> have the right response for everyone. (Col. 4:5-6 NLT)

How do we bring nonbelievers to Jesus? We become the positive influence they so desperately need. We would not know what we know about Jesus had someone not told us or demonstrated it to us.

> Always be joyful. Never stop praying. Be thankful in
> all circumstances, for this is God's will for you who
> belong to Christ Jesus. (1 Thess. 5:16–18 NLT)

If we are who we say we are in Christ and believe what we say we believe, our outward countenances should ooze with joy, our lips should never cease to call upon the Lord, and our hearts should be filled with unlimited thankfulness regardless of our situations.

Paul was the ultimate teacher, mentor, and encourager from beginning to end. This is what I most love about him. Paul not only started Christian churches, he started a relationship revolution. He didn't just plant a seed; he went back and checked on it as often as possible. If he couldn't get there physically, he wrote letters or sent someone in his place. His unwavering support of the early Christians was no doubt one of the biggest catalysts that caused their growth, and the Lord blessed this chain reaction. How incredibly excited Father God must have been as He watched Paul. How proud Jesus must have been to see Paul fully embrace his calling.

> For God is not unjust. He will not forget how hard you
> have worked for him and how you have shown your
> love to him by caring for other believers, as you still

> do. Our great desire is that you will keep on loving
> others as long as life lasts, in order to make certain
> that what you hope for will come true. Then you will
> not become spiritually dull and indifferent. Instead,
> you will follow the example of those who are going
> to inherit God's promises because of their faith and
> endurance. (Heb. 6:10–12 NLT)

This has become my focus. I want to be known only as a faithful follower of Christ. I want to be an incredible teacher, mentor, and encourager to all those around me. I want to have my Father in heaven say, "Well done, my good and faithful servant" (Matt. 25:21 NLT). How can I give Him any less?

On the other hand, if I simply say to myself that this is what I want to do, but don't put feet to it, nothing will materialize. There are three extremely important steps to realizing our dreams. The first step is to clearly define your aspiration. Write it out in as much detail as possible. Putting pen to paper is biblical and motivating.

> Then the LORD answered me and said: "Write the
> vision And make *it* plain on tablets, That he may run
> who reads it. For the vision *is* yet for an appointed
> time; But at the end it will speak, and it will not lie.
> Though it tarries, wait for it; Because it will surely
> come, It will not tarry." (Hab. 2:2–3 NKJV)

Second, speak your vision. Don't just pick anyone to share it with or share it randomly. Find someone who will provide sound advice, cheer you on, and hold you accountable. Lastly, pray to your heavenly Father and ask for His intervention every step of the way.

> The path to peace is paved with knee-prints. Bend
> the knee to His trustworthy authority. Surrender every

part of your life and every concern of your heart to the all-powerful, all-sufficient, all-knowing Creator of heaven and earth.—Beth Moore[1]

At the core point of my trial, Jesus would slowly begin to reveal a new plan for my life. Even now, I believe there are elements of the plan I have yet to be shown. I have pondered it; I have allowed it to reach the depths of my soul, but proactively I have written it. Here is my vision:

I would not be human if I said that I did not want to be vindicated for what was done to me. Nonetheless, because of what happened, I clearly see the veil that lies between this world around us and the spiritual one of God. It is clear to me, in a very real sense, how we walk (or should walk) separate from those of this world. And I can see the world and its trappings like no other time in my life.

I have for my entire nursing career helped those in physical pain, whether from cancer or noncancerous issues, and now I firmly feel led to help those with spiritual pain. Having experienced all that I did the last few years, I know how deeply one can hurt emotionally and mentally, yet I know a peace that surpasses all understanding. I have been journaling everything for quite some time along with all the Scriptures Chirst has given me. I know I am to put it in book form, but I have gotten away from it and need to get back to it. I know I need to birth this book.

I have a need from way down deep inside to take the last few years (not just some of it, but everything) and use it to help others so overwhelmed they feel alone in their sorrow, alone in their disappointment. I know there are speaking engagements I will be at someday, sharing my experiences. I see teaching the love of Christ in my future, not mainstream healthcare. Anyone with an interest in healthcare can train and provide medical care if they want, but not everyone will do what He needs them to do. I want to go where He needs me to go because I know I'll eventually help more people His way than the conventional way. Since working with pain patients, I have for the longest time seen the brokenness of this world, seen that behind the physical being are often complex spiritual issues that should be addressed. Funny, when we can't hide behind any physical cause of discomfort, we will even throw out mental or emotional labels before we dare to say the "S" word. Christ must truly be patient to put up with us!

My dilemma is simple. The struggles of this world overwhelm me at times! I know Jesus is building to something, and yet I feel the uncertainty of where it is going trying to weigh me down. I also know if my testimony is to be powerful and God-honoring; He is going to be the one that brings this whole open chapter full circle. As I wait, the time in between is nerve-racking! A friend and I were talking last night, and she said I was probably not quite ready yet, and Jesus was still working on me as well as behind the scenes to set the stage for what is to come. It makes a lot of sense. So I have the book *Sun Stand Still* and started reading it last night. As I go back to my Bible study and back to shaping my book, please pray for me for focus and drive! Thanks for listening!

After writing those words, I took the scariest step of all. I found two people in whom I could trust and sent it to them. Talk about frightening. Opening up is not easy. Allowing someone else to review your thoughts and feelings is intimidating. If you come to this point in the process, the Devil will fight you, and you have to be ready for the fallout. You can do this! There will be nothing more liberating than speaking your dreams to someone else.

> What, then, shall we say in response to these things?
> If God is for us, who can be against us? (Rom. 8:31 NIV)

Don't forget to pray! I prayed for focus, for direction, for the words He would have me to say. I prayed that He would keep my ego in check. I prayed that cover to cover He was glorified. Imagine my excitement as I found these words:

> I waited patiently for the LORD to help me, and he turned to me and heard my cry. He lifted me out of the pit of despair, out of the mud and the mire. He set my feet on solid ground and steadied me as I walked along. He has given me a new song to sing, a hymn of praise to our God. Many will see what he has done and be amazed. They will put their trust in the LORD. (Ps. 40:1–3 NLT)

Understand, Jesus is waiting to turn your life upside down. Can you see the vision? I pray you are open to the possibilities, and your heart is filled with a new song. Enjoy the journey. Trust in the Lord.

"For I know the plans I have for you," says the LORD. "They are plans for good and not for disaster, to give you a future and a hope."
—Jeremiah 29:11 (NLT)

CHAPTER 7

Have You Arrived Yet?
~Let's Talk~

The LORD keeps you from all harm and watches
over your life. The LORD keeps watch over you as
you come and go, both now and forever.
—Psalm 121:7–8 (NLT)

Can we take some time to look at your life? If you are not ready for such an exploration, you can come back when you are, but don't put it off too long. I hope you will choose to read on. For those who are continuing on, let me ask this: Are you in a true, authentic, interactive relationship with Jesus? If not, you need only to pray this simple prayer to establish that bond:

> Father God, I am seeking Your love and forgiveness. I want to receive Your grace and mercy. Forgive me of my sins. I acknowledge Your Son's birth, life, death, and resurrection. I ask Jesus to be my Lord and Savior. In Christ's name, I pray. Amen.

Now with that said, I encourage you to find a local church that will not only further your spiritual growth, but will also provide various opportunities to serve others regularly.

If you are a Christ follower, evaluate your current walk. Jesus used a very easy parable to explain the different types of people who attempt to follow Him.

> He told many stories in the form of parables, such as this one: "Listen! A farmer went out to plant some seeds. As he scattered them across his field, some seeds fell on a footpath, and the birds came and ate them. Other seeds fell on shallow soil with underlying rock. The seeds sprouted quickly because the soil was shallow. But the plants soon wilted under the hot sun, and since they didn't have deep roots, they died. Other seeds fell among thorns that grew up and choked out the tender plants. Still other seeds fell on fertile soil, and they produced a crop that was thirty, sixty, and even a hundred times as much as had been planted! Anyone with ears to hear should listen and understand." (Matt. 13:3–9 NLT)

Where do you see yourself in this story? If you are not growing in fertile soil, are there some changes you need to make? Know this is not a judgment. I have been there; we all have. Fully recognizing our need for Him in everything we do is the first step to true freedom.

Are you distracted from following Jesus as closely as you would like due to either a painful situation or a deep-seated fear? Remember pain and fear are the two biggest things that the Enemy is skilled at exploiting. Which emotion, if not both, is at the root of your current outlook? Let's dive a little deeper into those two issues.

> *Remember pain and fear are the two biggest things that the Enemy is skilled at exploiting.*

Work Through the Pain

I want you to truly believe Jesus understands like no other the depth of your pain as well as the lessons learned from it. I want to give you a verse to meditate on, and I hope it will sink deep within your heart.

> While Jesus was here on earth, he offered prayers and pleadings, *with a loud cry and tears*, to the one who could rescue him from death. And God heard his prayers because of his deep reverence for God. Even though Jesus was God's Son, *he learned obedience from the things he suffered.* (Heb. 5:7–8 NLT, italics mine)

We have an awesome Savior! In love for us, He suffered like us and beyond. We can trust Him with our hurts, sorrows, and disappointments. We can tell Him all the things weighing us down, and He will use it.

> Those expressions of desperation you feel so awful about are in fact the exact truth that God has been trying to bring to your attention. You flat out *don't* have the resources. He wants you to come to the place where you get before Him in a deeper way and tell Him what He's known to be true all along: you are in way over your head.
>
> God is taking you to a new level of dependence, and He *knows* what He's doing.—James MacDonald[1]

When we hand the situation over to Jesus and allow Him to comfort us, He helps us find meaning and purpose despite the situation. I love Jerry Bridges' perspective on pain in his book *Transforming Grace*:

> God never allows pain without a purpose in the lives of His children. He never allows Satan, nor circumstances, nor any ill-intending person to afflict us unless He uses that affliction for our good. God never wastes pain. He always causes it to work together for our ultimate good, the good of conforming us more to the likeness of His Son (see Rom. 8:28–29).[2]

There is no life more loving, more honest, or more fulfilling than the fully engaged Christian life. God has given us the keys to this life in His Word.

> The purpose of my instruction is that all believers would be filled with love that comes from a pure heart, a clear conscience, and genuine faith. (1 Tim. 1:5 NLT)

Conquering Your Fears

We all have fears. Some are small, and some are gigantic in nature. In 2003, when hurricane Isabelle came through our area of Virginia, my son was five years old and quite brave for his age. He didn't really know true fear. Isabelle would change that. During the storm, we had multiple trees fall in the yard, one squarely on my son's playset. He was unfazed. Then it happened; two trees fell straight toward the house, landing on the corner of our roof. In a matter of seconds, my child became afraid. The look on his face was unmistakable, and his body language expressed what was going on inside. The crash was loud, but fortunately, the physical damage was minimal. We recovered from the storm, but it has not been forgotten.

The Bible tells of another storm, one involving the disciples at sea. After having just fed more than five thousand people, Jesus sends the disciples away by boat while He stays behind to pray. While they are crossing the lake, the disciples encounter hard winds that threaten to capsize the boat. They are struggling to get to shore. Then Jesus comes walking across the water. They shrink in fear. Once Jesus identifies Himself, this conversation occurs:

> Then Peter called to him, "Lord, if it's really you, tell me to come to you, walking on the water."
>
> "Yes, come," Jesus said.
>
> So Peter went over the side of the boat and walked on the water toward Jesus. But when he saw the strong wind and the waves, he was terrified and began to sink. "Save me, Lord!" he shouted.
>
> Jesus immediately reached out and grabbed him. "You have so little faith," Jesus said. "Why did you doubt me?" (Matt. 14:28–31 NLT)

Now, before we criticize Peter for not having enough faith to get all the way to Jesus, let's first remember that we have all fallen short.

> For all have sinned and fall short of the glory of God. (Rom. 3:23 NKJV)

Secondly, let's praise him, because after all, Peter was the only one to venture out of the boat. Then, before we explore the reason Peter started sinking, let's understand the symbolism of the boat. In his book, *If You Want to Walk on Water, You've Got to Get Out of the Boat,* John Ortberg gives us this insight:

Your boat is whatever represents safety and security to you apart from God himself. Your boat is whatever you are tempted to put your trust in, especially when life gets a little stormy. Your boat is whatever keeps you so comfortable that you don't want to give it up even if it's keeping you from joining Jesus on the waves. Your boat is whatever pulls you away from the high adventure of extreme discipleship.

Want to know what your boat is? Your fear will tell you.[3]

Did Peter conquer his fears by stepping out onto the water? Partially. Taking his eyes off Jesus unfortunately allowed fear to return as his senses engaged the sounds of crashing waves and the feel of strong winds. Peter didn't start to slip beneath the water because he lost his footing or his balance. What he lost was his focus. When we are fearful, we focus on the wrong thing. When we focus on the circumstances, we don't see the solution. When we focus on the argument, we don't see the other person. When we focus on the fear, we don't see the Savior.

Fear comes from our enemy. He lobs smoke bombs at us constantly, each time hoping that we'll mistake it for a live grenade.—Craig Groeschel[4]

The Scriptures tell us repeatedly not to be afraid. God does not want you to be afraid; He wants you fearless.

For God has not given us a spirit of fear and timidity, but of power, love, and self-disciple. (2 Tim. 1:7 NLT)

Forward and fear can't coexist. You can't move forward until fear is in the rearview mirror.

During the storms that wreaked havoc on my life, I, like Peter, momentarily took my eyes off Jesus. We are all human; it will happen to each of us. Pain and fear take over in these times. Regardless, with each crashing wave, my focus grew stronger. I am no longer a storm watcher. My focus is directed squarely at the object of my faith—Jesus. Now when the storms of life come, I can see the Son still shining. In Matthew 14, verse 27 (NLT), Jesus states, "I am here!" Let these words resound in your mind. We must be confident and thoroughly convinced Jesus is always with us. He is with you when you go to work, when you get back home, when you sleep, and when you wake up. Even in times of pain or fear, He is there. Will you reach for His hand and allow Him to pull you up?

> "This is my command—be strong and courageous!
> Do not be afraid or discouraged. For the LORD your
> God is with you wherever you go." (Josh. 1:9 NLT)

When one truly steps back from the issues at hand and reviews Jesus' ministry, one discovers that His entire existence here on earth was filled with moments of relieving pain and calming fears. Jesus continues to be in the business of rescue and restore. Keep your eyes on Him, for He is never more than a glance away.

Dear Child:

Yesterday may have been a day for Psalm 142:

> I cry aloud to the LORD; I lift up my voice to the
> LORD for mercy. I pour out before him my complaint;
> before him I tell my trouble. When my spirit grows
> faint within me, it is you who watch over my way. In
> the path where I walk people have hidden a snare for

me. Look and see, there is no one at my right hand; no one is concerned for me. I have no refuge; no one cares for my life.

I cry to you, LORD; I say, "You are my refuge, my portion in the land of the living."

Listen to my cry, for I am in desperate need; rescue me from those who pursue me, for they are too strong for me. Set me free from my prison, that I may praise your name. Then the righteous will gather about me because of your goodness to me. (Ps. 142:1–7 NIV)

Today may be a day for Psalm 1:

Blessed is the one who does not walk in step with the wicked or stand in the way that sinners take or sit in the company of mockers, but whose delight is in the law of the LORD, and who meditates on his law day and night. That person is like a tree planted by streams of water, which yields its fruit in season and whose leaf does not wither—whatever they do prospers. Not so the wicked! They are like chaff that the wind blows away. Therefore the wicked will not stand in the judgment, nor sinners in the assembly of the righteous. For the LORD watches over the way of the righteous, but the way of the wicked leads to destruction. (Ps. 1:1–6 NIV)

Tomorrow may be a day for Psalm 100:

Shout for joy to the LORD, all the earth. Worship the LORD with gladness; come before him with joyful songs. Know that the LORD is God. It is he who made us, and we are his; we are his people, the sheep of his pasture. Enter his gates with thanksgiving and his courts with praise; give thanks to him and praise his name. For the LORD is good and his love endures forever; his faithfulness continues through all generations. (Ps. 100:1–5 NIV)

For all those days in between, make time for Psalm 23:

The LORD is my shepherd, I lack nothing. He makes me lie down in green pastures, he leads me beside quiet waters, he refreshes my soul. He guides me along the right paths for his name's sake. Even though I walk through the darkest valley, I will fear no evil, for you are with me; your rod and your staff, they comfort me. You prepare a table before me in the presence of my enemies. You anoint my head with oil; my cup overflows. Surely your goodness and love will follow me all the days of my life, and I will dwell in the house of the LORD forever. (Ps. 23:1–6 NIV)

No matter which type of day you are going through, just remember that I am here!

Jesus

LORD, you are mine!
    I promise to obey your words!
With all my heart, I want your blessings.
    Be merciful as you promised.
I pondered the direction of my life,
    and I turned to follow your laws.
I will hurry, without delay,
    to obey your commands.
Evil people try to drag me into sin,
    but I am firmly anchored to your instructions.
I rise at midnight to thank you
    for your just regulations.
I am a friend to anyone who fears you—
    anyone who obeys your commandments.
O LORD, your unfailing love fills the earth;
    teach me your decrees.
You have done many good things for me, LORD,
    just as you promised.
I believe in your commands;
    now teach me good judgment and
    knowledge.
I used to wander off until you disciplined me;
    but now I closely follow your word.
You are good and do only good;
    teach me your decrees.
Arrogant people smear me with lies,
    but in truth I obey your commandments with
    all my heart.
Their hearts are dull and stupid,
    but I delight in your instructions.
My suffering was good for me,
    for it taught me to pay attention to your
    decrees.
Your instructions are more valuable to me
    than millions in gold and silver.
—Psalm 119:57–72 (NLT)

CHAPTER 8

Daddy's Girl
~An Example I Can Live By~

What he opens no one can shut,
and what he shuts no one can open.
—Revelation 3:7 (NIV)

How does my story end? I'm glad you asked. For three years, leaning on the arms of Jesus, I would fight to rebuild my life through struggle after struggle. I would learn things about myself and my Savior that would set me on the course I am on today. Then for another two years, I worked in the place He put me. Though it was different from my original career path, I was grateful for the provision He gave. I used every opportunity I could to shine His Light, and I learned to appreciate the journey I was on with Him. At times, something still nagged at me. I sensed there was more I needed to accomplish for Him, and I suspected the current season was heading toward its conclusion. Toward the end of the second half of my five-year journey, there was a time when the culmination of everything that had happened began to stir around in my spirit. Once again, I would cry out to Him in search of an answer to my suffering.

Anyone who has been through a major life change entertains the question of why. Simply saying to oneself, "I knew there was a reason" doesn't necessarily satisfy our human curiosity. Jesus doesn't mind the questions, but He can only bring the answers when we are truly listening. Hearing from the Lord does not equal listening to the Lord. Story after story in the Bible proves that fact. When I was ready to listen to Jesus, I realized how tired I had become from trying to rationalize everything myself.

> *Hearing from the Lord does not*
> *equal listening to the Lord.*

I needed a word from Christ because at those times, I became tired. I needed Him to strengthen me as only He can do. One morning on my drive to work, the lyrics to "Worn" would provide the words I needed to say to Him:

> *Let me see redemption win*
> *Let me know the struggle ends*
> *That You can mend a heart that's frail and torn*
> *I wanna know a song can rise*
> *From the ashes of a broken life*
> *And all that's dead inside can be reborn*
> *'Cause I'm worn*[1]

What a testament to how in our human attempts to carry on, we just wear out. Truly by His grace do we see another sunrise. So easily do we forget just how reliant we are on His mercy. That morning I would sing out those words with all that was in me. It was the prayer of my heart, and it translated all that was swirling around in my spirit. Jesus would answer me in the sweetest way.

But in that coming day no weapon turned against you will succeed. You will silence every voice raised up to accuse you. These benefits are enjoyed by the servants of the LORD; their vindication will come from me. I, the LORD, have spoken! (Isa. 54:17 NLT)

This is the promise that would come to me through one of my coworkers. Jesus would use someone who had been a witness to my nursing career for years. I have no doubt she was placed in my path that day to deliver a message from God. During a random visit to the department she worked in, she approached me. Note this is someone I would not see every day. In fact, we had not seen each other in weeks when this conversation took place. We had never discussed anything personal. I assumed it was a work-related issue. I was about to get the surprise of my life. She said,

I have been told to tell you, no weapon formed against you will ever prosper. You need to know that. When God is with us, He has us. When you were in pain management, you thought it was something good you were being led into, but it was not. You were carrying a burden too big for you, and you had to be removed from the situation so it would not consume you. It was too much and was slowly working to destroy you. It was taking too much from you, and you were not appreciated for what you were attempting to do. What you went through looked like it would kill you, but you are able to overcome it. Everything will be okay. It doesn't matter what was said about you. We may wonder why we have to go through such things, but it is to strengthen us. What you were put through was to strengthen you. I know what kind of person you are and the kind of nurse you have been. I remember

when you first started out in nursing school. You will
be fine. I just needed to tell you that today.

Talk about your jaw-dropping moments! Instantly, I had chills
and almost started balling my eyes out. Here was the answer
to my struggles. The God of the universe just reached out and
spoke into my life. Utterly amazing! Forever are those words
burned into my heart.

> He will make your innocence radiate like the dawn,
> and the justice of your cause will shine like the
> noonday sun. (Ps. 37:6 NLT)

A short time afterwards, Jesus began shifting my life around
again. The company I was working for had been bought out
a couple of months earlier, and within the merger process,
positions were beginning to be cut. Try as he might, the Devil
could whisper in my ear all he wanted; I was not taking the
bait. This time I could be confident that wherever life took me,
Jesus was present and in control. While events unfolded, I took
the time to process everything all over again with the purpose
of looking forward. I recommitted to my vision, and this book
would begin to be born. As I began this project, Jesus would
reveal the start of a dream opening my eyes to what He was
accomplishing. I don't want you to miss this! He can do the
same for you.

Let's explore the true beginning of my God story. Nine years
into my past, I felt a calling. I didn't fully realize it to be a calling,
but I knew Jesus was pulling at my heartstrings. I came to a
place in life where I hungered for Christ to reveal Himself to me.
I wanted to fully engage this Savior I said I believed in. Over a
two-year period, I would dive into God's Word, I would listen to
numerous sermons by numerous pastors and teachers, I would
consume book after book, I would read the Bible in its entirety,

and as a family, we would be guided to a new church home. Back then, I am certain I had no earthly idea what I was really asking. I certainly had no concept of how He would answer.

> "Ask and it will be given to you; seek and you will find; knock and the door will be opened to you." (Matt. 7:7 NIV)

Only now in hindsight do I see how everything came full circle:

- a simple cry out to my Savior—to know Him, to be used by Him, and to experience His fullness;
- an urge to break from legalism and tradition, freeing my soul;
- sound teaching and instruction to build my faith;
- fiery trail (refinement) to prepare me for service;
- revelation of the one true mission;
- enlightenment of an answer to prayer; and
- positioned for service.

How could I have missed it? The journey from seeking Him, to knowing Him, to being used by Him just happened! Jesus heard my prayer of so many years ago and answered it. Realizing how He put the puzzle pieces together and knowing all the hard times were allowed to bring me into line with His perfect will for my life leaves no room for doubt to exist. When He moves, we need only to trust, and He will bring the answers in due time.

As the job cuts continued to surface, I learned my position was being terminated. As I left on my last day of employment, I began to praise Jesus for what He was about to do. I would not fall victim to the Devil's mind games, not this time. Four weeks later, I received a job offer from a successful company that enabled me to work from home. I would take a position that allowed my full skill set to be used, and it would set us on a financial course that would replace all the Devil had stolen. It was nothing short of spectacular. This is my Jesus. I stand in awe of Him; I stand in amazement of Him; I stand forever changed and so very grateful that this is just the beginning.

> When the Savior calls you out of something, sometimes He calls you all the way out.

This is the true Christian walk. It is not for the faint of heart, and it is life transformation at its finest. Are you walking with the one true God? Does the process intimidate you? Don't let it. Everyone's walk with Chirst is unique to them, but the process remains the same. How long you stay at each level depends on how much you dig in. You will repeat the process over and over, but the first time through will be the most memorable. God is a loving Father who sent His only Son to show you the way. He would love nothing more than to have a relationship with you, to help you grow, to bless you. He wants nothing more than to add you to His A-list of kids who have done great things. He wants to be there when you take your first steps, He wants to hold your hand when you cry, and He wants to celebrate your victories with you. He is forever calling out—do you hear Him?
He is forever reaching out—do you feel Him?

> Understand, therefore, that the LORD your God is indeed God. He is the faithful God who keeps his covenant for a thousand generations and lavishes his unfailing love on those who love him and obey his commands. (Deut. 7:9 NLT)

Christ longs to redeem our lives, to set us apart. Redemption, defined by Jesus, is an acknowledgement of who we belong to, not what we have done. Further, redemption doesn't assess our real values, but multiplies our worths. When we discover worldly recognition is fleeting, but redemption through Jesus is everlasting, life takes on a completely new dimension.

> *Redemption, defined by Jesus, is an*
> *acknowledgement of who we belong*
> *to, not what we have done.*

Never be afraid to start over, be afraid of standing still too long.

And what do you benefit if you gain the whole world but lose your own soul? Is anything worth more than your soul? (Matt. 16:26 NLT)

Moses' life, seen in the book of Exodus, is a great example of Jesus leading us to start over in order to fulfill our destinies. When he was a Hebrew baby, he was taken from his traditional Jewish home and raised by Egyptian royalty. Unfortunately, an overzealous effort to correct a wrong would turn into a destructive situation, forcing him to leave Egypt. In stark contrast to his former life, he would lead a lowly and humble existence, never once suspecting one day God would come calling. Then, without warning, Moses would come face to face with Yahweh in the form of a burning bush. God spoke to Moses, and even in the awe of the moment, with such a wondrous sight before him, Moses would recoil into the recesses of his own self-image.

"Look! The cry of the people of Israel has reached me, and I have seen how harshly the Egyptians abuse them. Now go, for I am sending you to Pharaoh. You must lead my people Israel out of Egypt." But

> Moses protested to God, "Who am I to appear before Pharaoh? Who am I to lead the people of Israel out of Egypt?" (Ex. 3:9–11 NLT)

Moses would question and challenge the Lord's decision, immediately shutting down inside due to his own perceptions. God would counter Moses' stance, firmly nudging him on. Moses' mind must have been racing; the questions would start piling up. Three times Moses would offer the Lord excuses for why this plan would not work: the people of Israel would need proof of who sent him; the people of Israel would not be easily satisfied with mere words; and lastly, his version of the Lord's instructions would end up distorted or confused. God would not be persuaded. Out of excuses, Moses would beg, "Lord, please! Send anyone else" (Ex. 4:13 NLT). Moses was simply afraid; he had been standing still too long. He allowed the pain and fear of his past to cloud his ability to dream again. Even so, God would not allow him to remain stuck. Moses would indeed lead the children of Israel out of bondage and at the same time break the chains that once controlled him.

As we wrap up our time together, let me leave you with some points to think over.

- Most of what we perceive to be important is not on God's list of priorities.
- No one is more brilliant than the person who realizes he or she is thoughtless without Him.
- The true start of our lives begins only after we release all we envision and allow Jesus to give us His vision.
- Contemplation of what others think of us allows us to become boxed in. Seeing ourselves as Jesus sees us is ultimate freedom.

- What we perceive as punishment is only the beginning of Christ showing grace and mercy, for there is no end to His love.
- No one has ever found true happiness outside of Him, but many have settled for manufactured contentment without Him.
- How we view this world begins to brighten when we see it as the Creator intended it to be.
- No amount of education can prepare someone for his or her biggest and most important career in life—to love others.
- No matter where it starts, our relative worths and fortunes in life begin to rise when we see what others in real need look like.
- Jesus was the true author of taking a stand, and I for one strive to stand humbly with Him, yet boldly for Him.

As this chapter closes, know this:

I have not stopped thanking God for you. I pray for you constantly, asking God, the glorious Father of our Lord Jesus Christ, to give you spiritual wisdom and insight so that you might grow in your knowledge of God. I pray that your hearts will be flooded with light so that you can understand the confident hope he has given to those he called—his holy people who are his rich and glorious inheritance. I also pray that you will understand the incredible greatness of God's power for us who believe him. This is the same mighty power that raised Christ from the dead and seated him in the place of honor at God's right hand in the heavenly realms. (Eph. 1:16–20 NLT)

Call out to Him, and love will echo back.

The wife of a man from the company of the prophets cried out to Elisha, "Your servant my husband is dead, and you know that he revered the LORD. But now his creditor is coming to take my two boys as his slaves." Elisha replied to her, "How can I help you? Tell me, what do you have in your house?" "Your servant has nothing there at all," she said, "except a small jar of olive oil."

Elisha said, "Go around and ask all your neighbors for empty jars. Don't ask for just a few. Then go inside and shut the door behind you and your sons. Pour oil into all the jars, and as each is filled, put it to one side."

She left him and shut the door behind her and her sons. They brought the jars to her and she kept pouring. When all the jars were full, she said to her son, "Bring me another one." But he replied, "There is not a jar left." Then the oil stopped flowing.

She went and told the man of God, and he said, "Go, sell the oil and pay your debts. You and your sons can live on what is left."

—2 Kings 4:1–7 (NIV)

CONCLUSION

~The Widow's Oil~

God is not a man, so he does not lie. He is not
human, so he does not change his mind. Has
he ever spoken and failed to act? Has he ever
promised and not carried it through?
—Numbers 23:19 (NLT)

I love the story of the widow's oil for many different reasons. Many people can relate to her story as she is caught in the crossfire of life. In her distress, she reaches out for help from an external source—Elisha. However, Elisha turns the tables on her and inquires: "Tell me, what do you have in your house?" (2 Kings 4:2 NIV). She is skeptical about her worth, but in passing mentions that she has a little oil.

At first glance, this story could be taken as just another illustration of someone's financial needs being met. The real problem, in fact, is faith. God, through Elisha, is about to demonstrate that all anyone ever has is little in nature, but with faith, God can use what we have to fill a big need. We don't need to turn our focuses outward. The answers we are seeking have already been placed inside us, and they become evident when our faith is used.

> *God, through Elisha, is about to demonstrate that all anyone ever has is little in nature, but with faith, God can use what we have to fill a big need.*

The other element of the story worth mentioning is Elisha's instruction on gathering jars. He states, "Don't ask for just a few" (2 Kings 4:3 NIV). God is seeking those who will be bold enough to pray real God-sized prayers. If He promises it, He can and will deliver. We need only to ask according to His will.

Lastly, notice that without hesitation, the widow follows Elisha's instructions. She is catching a vision. How appropriate is her reaction when the jars are full. She asks for more jars. God loves to reward this kind of expectancy. Not only does the widow believe He will meet her need; she believes He will exceed it.

> What you see as small and insignificant, is the very thing the Lord may choose to use. All it takes is faith.
>
> So do not throw away this confident trust in the LORD. Remember the great reward it brings you! Patient endurance is what you need now, so that you will continue to do God's will. Then you will receive all that he has promised. (Heb. 10:35–36 NLT)

I have heard it said that during your lowest points and your darkest moments, God is working on setting up a victory you never imagined. You still have a little something left. Don't get lost in the silence. Listen for the footsteps of God!

Notes

Chapter 1
Spiritual Oz: This Isn't Kansas

1. "Easing chronic pain: Better treatments and medications." *NIH MedlinePlus.* 2007 Fall; 2(4): 20. http://www.nlm.nih.gov/medlineplus/magazine/issues/fall07/articles/fall07pg20.html (June 2, 2014).
2. Lucado, Max. *Cure for the Common Life: Living in Your Sweet Spot.* Nashville, TN: Thomas Nelson Inc., 2005, p. 1.

Chapter 2
When the Rain Lasts All Day and All Night: Your Hair Will Be Frizzy

1. Camp, Jeremy. (2008). There Will Be A Day. On *Speaking louder than before* [CD]. Seattle, WA: BEC Recordings.
2. "Testimony." *Merriam-Webster.com:* http://www.merriam-webster.com/dictionary/testimony (February 9, 2014).
3. Lewis, C.S. (Hooper, Walter, Ed.). *The Collected Letters of C. S. Lewis, Volume 3: Nania, Cambridge, and Joy 1950-1963.* New York, NY: HarperCollins Publishing, 2007, p. 106.
4. Camp, *op.cit.*
5. Third Day. (2005). Mountain of God. On *Wherever you are* [CD]. Franklin, TN: Essential Records.

Chapter 4
The Road Less Traveled: And All I Packed Was High Heel Shoes

1. Noble, Perry. "Unstoppable Journey." Sermon series *One Prayer,* presented via Internet at Believers Church, Chesapeake, VA. June 2010.

2. Stuart, Jamey. "Unstoppable Plan." Sermon series *One Prayer*, presented at Believers Church, Chesapeake, VA. June 2010.

3. Stuart, Jamey. "Developing Audacious Faith." Sermon series *Sun Stand Still*, presented at Believers Church, Chesapeake, VA. April 2011.

4. Furtick, Steven. *Sun Sand Still: What Happens When You Dare to Ask God for the Impossible.* Colorado Spings, CO: Multnomah Books, 2010.

5. Furtick, *op.cit.*, p. 54.

6. Stuart, 2011, *op.cit.*

Chapter 6
Are We There Yet?: Enough Said

1. Moore, Beth. *Breaking Free, Updated edition: The Journey, The Stories.* Nashville, TN: Lifeway Press, (1999) 2010, p. 49.

Chapter 7
Have You Arrived Yet?: Let's Talk

1. MacDonald, James. *When Life Is Hard.* Chicago, IL: Moody Publishers, 2010, pp. 30–31.

2. Bridges, Jerry. *Transforming Grace: Living Confidently in God's Unfailing Love.* Colorado Springs, CO: Navpress Publishing, 2008, p. 139.

3. Ortberg, John. *If You Want to Walk on Water, You've Got to Get Out of the Boat.* Grand Rapids, MI: Zondervan, 2001, p. 17.

4. Groeschel, Craig. *Soul Detox: Clean Living in a Contaminated World.* Grand Rapids, MI: Zondervan, 2012, p. 146.

Chapter 8
Daddy's Girl: An Example I Can Live By

1. Tenth Avenue North. (2012). Worn. On *The struggle* [CD]. Nashville, TN: Sony/ATV Music Publishing LLC.

MESSAGE FROM THE AUTHOR

I sincerely hope you have enjoyed *Love Echoed Back* as much as I have enjoyed sharing it with you. I would love to hear the insights Jesus has revealed to you through this book. If something has touched you deeply, feel free to reach out and tell me about it.

You may contact me one of three ways:

My Blog: www.elainelankford.com
My Facebook page:
https://www.facebook.com/LoveEchoedBack
My Twitter account: Elaine A Lankford @loveechoedback

I look forward to hearing from you!
Elaine